colour
reflexology
for health & healing

colour reflexology

for health & healing

pauline wills

vega

Acknowledgements
My thanks go to my sister, Patricia Jackson, and Alison Moss for their editorial
assistance, and to Andrew Easton for his design skills.

ISBN 1-84333-018-0

A catalogue record for this book is available from the British Library.

First published in 2002 by
Vega
64 Brewery Road
London, N7 9NT

A member of **Chrysalis** Books plc

visit our website at www.chrysalisbooks.co.uk

Designed by Design Revolution
Production by Susan Sutterby

Printed in Slovenia

Contents

Foreword

Due to my work as president of the Complementary Medical Association and the work that I undertake in my role as broadcaster and writer, I am in the incredibly privileged position of being able to be kept at the forefront of developments within the entire field of complementary medicine. I have to read extensively as part of my work and much of the literature that comes across my desk is of great quality but is, ultimately, a re-working of many previous therapeutic approaches and theories.

Once in a while a true innovator comes along, in this case Pauline Wills. Pauline works tirelessly to push forward therapeutic boundaries. While there are many practitioners who work hard, developing and moving complementary medicine forward, Pauline is always concerned with 'quality control', that is, she is constantly evolving, while maintaining the very highest standards of practice. This is of utmost importance, as anyone working in complementary medicine will realize that we are working in an area that is easily 'marginalized' by the conventional medical fraternity and the pharmaceutical industry on the largely unfounded basis that the work that many of us do is 'unscientific'.

This accusation is levelled at us for many reasons, not least of which is that most of those working in the field of 'science' have some vested interest on some level of their work. This is of course one of the many reasons that so many complementary medical techniques are still not accepted as mainstream, viable medical interventions.

Similar to women working in a predominantly male environment, in order to be respected we have to exceed the base line standards set by the majority – in this case the conventional medical profession. With Pauline Wills' adherence to standards of excellence, I believe she does go 'that extra mile'. Her books are thorough; her training courses are lengthy and rigorous. Her graduates are respected throughout the complementary medical industry. Pauline Wills garners respect in every area of her work.

This book is well thought out and beautifully executed. Furthermore, due to Pauline's clear teaching style, the ideas set out here are easily accessible and assimilable into one's practice from the start. The ideas put forward are thoroughly researched and drawn from the very best sources of information available in the field of light and colour research today. The content is extremely useful to practitioners working in a multitude of disciplines, since light and colour are intrinsic to our well-being. I foresee that while this book is directed at practitioners of colour reflexology, it should also serve as recommended reading for students of other complementary medical disciplines. It will certainly feature on the Complementary Medical Association's 'Highly Recommended' books list.

Jayney Goddard
June 2002

Reflexology and Colour

Introduction

My journey into the realm of complementary therapy began many years ago. It started with the study of yoga, at a time when it was not widely known. Looking back I appreciate how fortunate I was to be taught by an Indian master who had devoted most of his life to its study and practice. Yoga philosophy taught me about the chakras or energy centres situated in our aura and the colours that these radiate. For me, the most fascinating aspect of this philosophy was the realization that we are beings of light, surrounded and interpenetrated by the colours that constitute light. I longed to know more.

Healing with colour

Several years later, the chance to increase my colour knowledge came when I saw an advertisement in the local library for courses on colour therapy, to be held at the Maitreya School of Colour Healing in London. I enrolled for the course and, with great enthusiasm, began an exploration into the fascinating world of colour.

Among a wealth of interesting information, the course detailed the properties relating to the spectral colours and demonstrated how these could be applied in a healing context. It explored our subtle anatomy and showed how the aura is determined by our emotional, mental and physical well-being. But what the course did most for me was to make me look at myself and how my life was patterned by conditioning, most of which was not relevant. This conditioning had created barriers that now needed to be slowly dismantled if I wanted to heal myself and start to flow with the energies of life. This was, and still is, hard (and at times very painful) work, but I do believe that if we are unable to heal ourselves then we are not able to help others. Ultimately, the only person who can heal is the one to whom the disease belongs: practitioners, as channels for healing, act as catalyst and sounding board for the person who is working to heal her- or himself. At the end of the colour course I worked alongside Lily Cornford, one of the founders of the Maitreya School. Under her expert guidance, and not without reprimand, I gained practical experience in applying what had been taught.

Shortly after qualifying as a colour practitioner I trained to become a reflexologist, feeling that the combination of yoga, colour and reflexology would provide both a firm foundation for working with myself and the necessary skills for working with other people. Having qualified, I worked as a colour practitioner and reflexologist until eventually I felt it was time to impart to others the knowledge gained over the years.

It was while travelling abroad to conduct an introductory course on colour's vibrational energies that the idea of integrating colour with reflexology came to mind. This supplied much food for thought. I had no idea how this integration could be achieved. Were the two therapies compatible? And were there any benefits to be derived from combining them?

Combining the two therapies

On returning home, I began experimenting on myself with the combination of these two therapies. What I ultimately discovered was that colour enhanced a reflexology treatment and eased conditions that are difficult to treat with reflexology on its own: using colour worked not just with the physical ailment but also with the emotional and mental aspects of the person being treated.

Another benefit was that colour could break down accumulated energy painlessly. During a reflexology treatment, a painful reflex is indicative of either a physically manifested disease or an accumulation of stagnant energy in the aura. It might also show that the part of the body related to this reflex is working extra hard – normally due to impaired functioning of one or more of the body's organs – to help keep the person in a state of homeostasis. The recommended treatment for painful reflexes is to apply specific compression techniques in order to clear the stagnant energy. This can be a very uncomfortable procedure and has deterred many people from seeking further treatment. However,

the application of the correct colour can achieve this energy dispersion painlessly. I also discovered that the application of colour to certain reflexes induces a state of complete relaxation. This is very beneficial if applied at the start of a treatment because a relaxed body is able to assimilate healing energies more effectively.

About the book

Through the research carried out on myself and my family I was able to formulate a pattern for treatment combining the two therapies – a pattern which constantly changes as I myself grow and gather more information. After several years of working with, and treating clients with, reflexology and colour, I began to share my discoveries with other reflexologists.

The aim of this book is to open up the wonderful healing power of colour; to give information for self-help and to act as a source of reference for reflexologists wishing to integrate these two therapies. What I must stress is that anyone suffering any form of illness should always seek medical advice and not work solely from the information given in this book. I would also like to say that no book can replace 'hands on' experience, and we always recommend that reflexologists wishing to integrate colour with reflexology attend a recognized course which contains a required number of practical modules.

The History of Reflexology

Reflexology, or zone therapy as it is sometimes called, is a very ancient therapy the origin of which is unknown. There is speculation that it originated from the Incas, dating back to 12,000 BC. They, at a later date, passed their knowledge of zone therapy to the North American Indians who, it is believed, continue to use it. Another theory places its origin in Egypt. This idea stems from an Egyptian tomb drawing dating back to 2,330 BC. The drawing shows four people; one is being treated with hand massage and another with foot massage.

Another conjecture, afforded by Dr William Fitzgerald in his book *Zone Therapy*, is that reflexology was acknowledged in India and China some 5,000 years ago. What is certain is that reflexology was used by the great Florentine Sculptor, Cellini (1500–71) to relieve physical pain. Likewise, US President Garfield (1831–81) is reported to have alleviated the pain of an assassination attempt by applying pressure to specific parts of his feet.

During the sixteenth century several books were published in Europe on zone therapy. Dr A Tatis and Dr Adamus wrote the first of these. Shortly afterwards a similar book, written by Dr Bell, appeared in Leipzig. During the nineteenth century Dr Bressler published an important book on zone therapy. It was an account of his research into linking the pressure points on the feet with the internal organs of the physical body. It was Bressler's research that Dr Fitzgerald (the man accredited for initiating reflexology in its present form) studied.

The development of reflexology techniques

Dr Fitzgerald was born in Middletown, USA, in 1872 and died in Stamford, USA in 1942. In 1895 he graduated in medicine at the University of Vermont and then practised in hospitals in Vienna, Paris and London before specializing in ear, nose and throat disorders.

After studying the work of Bressler, he started to practise zone therapy techniques on his patients. His method of treatment was to apply pressure to specific parts of the foot using probes, clamps and rubber bands. He discovered that, when these were applied, anaesthesia was induced in specific parts of the body.

Fitzgerald's continuing research was publicly described in 1916 by Dr E Bowers, who named it Zone Therapy. This name probably arose from Fitzgerald's work on formulating the body into ten equal longitudinal zones (see page 12). In 1917 Fitzgerald and Bowers published their work in the book *Zone Therapy*. This book contained recommendations and therapeutic proposals for doctors, dentists, chiropractors and ear, nose and throat specialists. It contained diagrams of the reflexes found on the feet and the corresponding division of the ten longitudinal zones of the body. Fitzgerald's work was not well received by the medical profession in general, but a Dr Joseph Shelby Riley and his wife – also a doctor – were so impressed by what they read that they enrolled for one of Fitzgerald's courses, to enable them to incorporate his teachings on zone therapy into their own work. It was an assistant of Joseph Riley, Eunice Ingham (1879–1974), who developed reflexology into its present form.

Eunice Ingham was an American masseuse. Her contribution to reflexology was her research in correlating the anatomical structure of the body with the energy zones on the feet. Through this work she discovered that the feet provided a mirror image of the entire body. She also developed a special subtle method of massage – the Ingham method of compression massage – for use with reflexology. This is described in her first published book *Stories The Feet Can Tell*. Her second book is called *Stories The Feet Have Told*.

Eunice Ingham spent much time travelling in order to share her knowledge with other therapists. In 1960 Doreen Bayly, one of her students, introduced reflexology to England, where she started a reflexology training school.

A modern-day therapy

Today, reflexology is credited with a greater scientific background based on our growing knowledge of anatomy and physiology. This has helped its acceptance into conventional,

orthodox medicine. Reflexologists are welcomed in many palliative care centres and reflexology is practised in some hospitals. Unfortunately, most of this work is on a voluntary basis, which I feel discredits the profession by failing to honour the professionalism of the practitioner.

Since its introduction into the United Kingdom, reflexology has continued to evolve both in its methods and techniques. There is now vertical reflexology, treating the meridians on the hands and feet in conjunction with a reflexology treatment; the integration of sound with reflexology – the work of Olivea Dewhurst-Maddock; and the integration of the vibrational energies of colour with reflexology, the theme of this book.

On several occasions I have heard it said that reflexology should be kept pure and not integrated with other therapies. It is my opinion that each person is an individual whose response to various therapies is unique. During my years working with the integration of reflexology and colour, I have found people who greatly benefit from the combination of the two therapies. At the Oracle School of Colour, we run courses for qualified reflexologists who wish to work with the vibrational energy of colour on the reflexes on the hands or the feet. Our aim is to provide participants with a variety of ways of working with the integration of these two therapies, to enable them to formulate an individual treatment procedure for each patient.

The Longitudinal and Transverse Zones

Reflexology teaches that a vital energy called life force, prana or chi circulates in a balanced, rhythmic way between all the organs of the body and permeates every living cell. Bacterial and virus-related diseases, among others, can upset the energy balance in the body causing stagnation and energy blocks. When this vital energy stagnates over and around a specific organ and in the corresponding part of the aura, the organ suffers disease.

The Ten Longitudinal Zones

The human system, functioning in accordance with the law of polarity, has two main points, one at the top of the head and one at the feet. The point at the top of the head is receptive to spiritual energies and the point at the feet works primarily as a receptor for body consciousness, differentiation of earth energies and the release of earth energies. Between these two main points lie the ten equal longitudinal zones formulated by Dr Fitzgerald. There are five zones in each half of the body; they lie between the head and the toes and the five fingers. Within these zones are found all the muscles and organs of the physical body.

Because both feet and both hands are a mirror image of the body, these zones are mirrored on them.

THE TEN LONGITUDINAL ZONES ON THE BODY

THE TEN LONGITUDINAL ZONES ON THE FEET

The Transverse Zones

The body, and therefore the feet, can be further divided into three transverse zones. (On the hands, because of the position of the thumb, only the middle transverse zone is shown.) The inclusion of the three transverse zones was the work of German reflexologist Hanne Marquarett, author of *Reflex Zone Therapy of the Feet*. She felt that their inclusion with the longitudinal zones would make the feet into a miniature map, thus facilitating greater precision in locating the reflexes.

The first transverse zone lies between the phalanges and the metatarsal bones. Above this are found the reflexes to the head and the neck. The second transverse zone lies between the metatarsals, the cuneiform and the cuboid bones. Above this are found the reflexes to the chest and upper abdomen. The third transverse zone lies midway between the calcaneus and the talus bone. Above this are the reflexes to the abdomen and pelvis.

THE TRANSVERSE ZONES ON THE FOOT

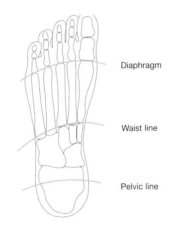

Diaphragm

Waist line

Pelvic line

THE TRANSVERSE ZONES ON THE BODY AND THE FEET

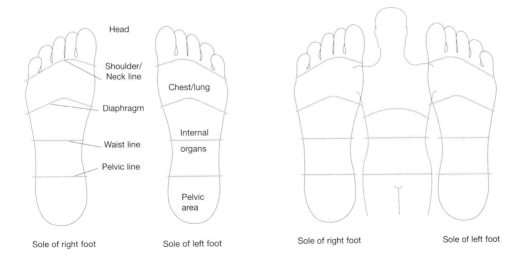

Head

Shoulder/
Neck line

Diaphragm

Waist line

Pelvic line

Chest/lung

Internal
organs

Pelvic
area

Sole of right foot

Sole of left foot

Sole of right foot

Sole of left foot

Energy blocks

Stagnation, or energy blocks, located in the zones and the aura can stem from our physical, mental or emotional self and can have many causes. These could include stress, an unbalanced diet, an unhealthy lifestyle, a broken marriage or relationship. If this stagnant energy is to be permanently eradicated then the cause for its presence has to be ascertained and worked with.

The role of the reflexologist

Helping the client to find and work with the cause of the problem can take many hours of counselling, a vital part of any therapy. It has been said that illness provides a great opportunity for spiritual growth and awareness at all levels of our being, but how many of us accept this opportunity for growth when we are ill.

Working in this way necessitates taking responsibility for our own health and not assuming that responsibility lies with our doctor. I do believe that conventional medicine has its place and can work hand in hand with complementary therapies but, whichever kind of therapy we choose, the responsibility for our health still lies with us.

With this in mind, a reflexology treatment should not be carried out as a purely mechanical therapy. During treatment the auras of patient and therapist come into contact. If therapists are sensitive to this contact they should be able to feel into the patient and detect the presence of any dis-harmony. This knowledge can be really helpful when assisting patients to re-harmonize themselves.

Each of us is a triple being, comprising body, mind and spirit and it is only when these three aspects are in harmony that we can become whole. All reflexology treatments should, therefore, be working with these three levels.

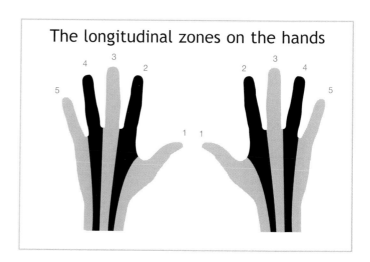

The longitudinal zones on the hands

Reflexes on the Feet and Hands

Assuming that readers interested in using colour with reflexology are already qualified reflexologists or are in training, I do not intend to go into great detail about the reflexes of the hands and feet and the methods of treating them. This subject has already been covered in many excellent books. What I have done, however, is include diagrams on the following pages of the feet and the hands, showing and naming the individual reflexes.

The soles of our feet and the palms of our hands are mirror images of the whole body because it is in them that energy terminates. The energy terminating on the feet is thought to be more powerful than that terminating on the hands, thus making it more beneficial to treat the feet. However, when using reflexology for self-help, it is easier to treat our hands.

When working on a person's feet or hands, we should allow healing energy to flow into them through our own hands. The earth energy enters our body through our feet, and the universal energy flows in through the crown of our head. Both these energies meet in the heart chakra where they are united in unconditional love. From the heart chakra this energy then flows down our arms, into our hands and fingers, to be transferred to the person we are working with.

Healing energy or prana originates from the sun and is found in abundance in our atmosphere on bright sunny days. Prana can be seen as brilliant white specks of light floating in the atmosphere. Each tiny speck contains all the spectral colours. When therapists work with colour, we take from light the colour needed by a person and transfer it to them either through the hands or the feet, using one of several methods. This will be explained further on page 47.

I have found it beneficial to begin a treatment with simple foot movements and a gentle massage to both feet. This accustoms the patient to the sensation of touch and induces a state of relaxation. It is easier to absorb energies if we are relaxed. Beginning on the right, I rotate each foot from the ankle joint and then gently rotate each toe. Care must be taken when using this technique on those suffering from joint disorders such as arthritis or osteoporosis. Always use your free hand to support the joints that you are rotating, and give your full attention to the task in hand to ensure that the joints suffer no undue strain. As well as inducing a relaxed state, these simple movements start to increase the energy flow in the patient. Rotating the big toe can frequently alleviate stiffness in a patient's neck.

During a reflexology treatment I prefer not to engage in conversation, so that my concentration does not lose its focus. However, if patients choose to talk, I allow them to do so. Often, the therapist is the only person a patient is able to talk to, and to deny this could hinder the healing process.

To complete a reflexology treatment, I always massage both feet before applying any colour. I find this relaxes the patient, especially if there has been some discomfort.

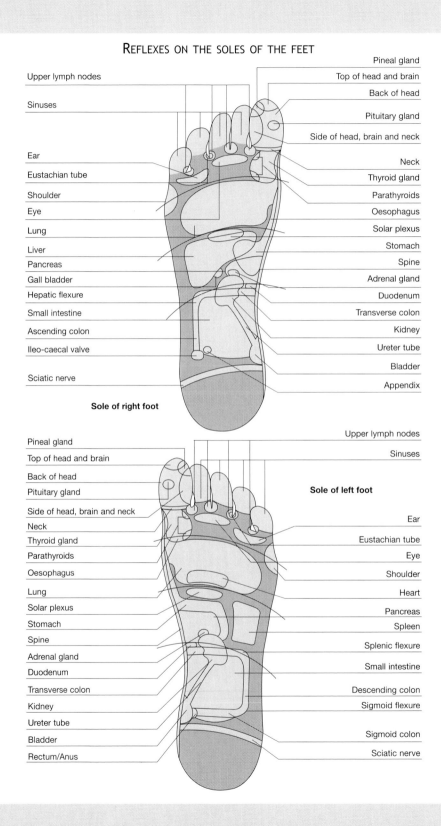

REFLEXES ON THE SOLES OF THE FEET

Upper lymph nodes

Sinuses

Ear

Eustachian tube

Shoulder

Eye

Lung

Liver

Pancreas

Gall bladder

Hepatic flexure

Small intestine

Ascending colon

Ileo-caecal valve

Sciatic nerve

Pineal gland

Top of head and brain

Back of head

Pituitary gland

Side of head, brain and neck

Neck

Thyroid gland

Parathyroids

Oesophagus

Solar plexus

Stomach

Spine

Adrenal gland

Duodenum

Transverse colon

Kidney

Ureter tube

Bladder

Appendix

Sole of right foot

Pineal gland

Top of head and brain

Back of head

Pituitary gland

Side of head, brain and neck

Neck

Thyroid gland

Parathyroids

Oesophagus

Lung

Solar plexus

Stomach

Spine

Adrenal gland

Duodenum

Transverse colon

Kidney

Ureter tube

Bladder

Rectum/Anus

Upper lymph nodes

Sinuses

Sole of left foot

Ear

Eustachian tube

Eye

Shoulder

Heart

Pancreas

Spleen

Splenic flexure

Small intestine

Descending colon

Sigmoid flexure

Sigmoid colon

Sciatic nerve

REFLEXES ON THE TOP OF THE FEET

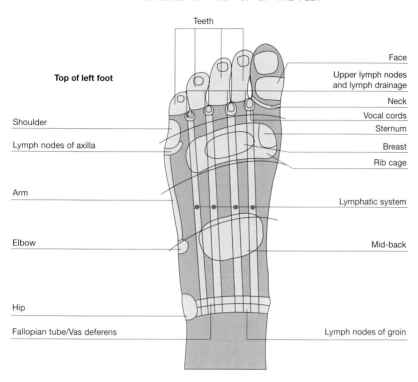

Teeth

Top of left foot

Face
Upper lymph nodes and lymph drainage
Neck
Vocal cords
Sternum
Breast
Rib cage

Shoulder

Lymph nodes of axilla

Arm

Lymphatic system

Elbow

Mid-back

Hip

Fallopian tube/Vas deferens

Lymph nodes of groin

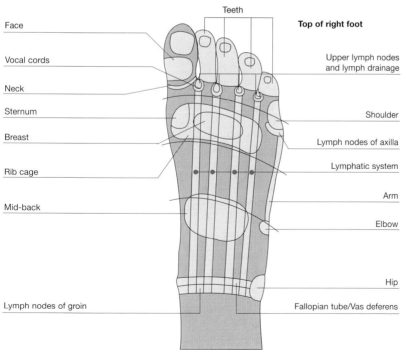

Teeth

Top of right foot

Face

Vocal cords

Neck

Sternum

Breast

Rib cage

Mid-back

Lymph nodes of groin

Upper lymph nodes and lymph drainage

Shoulder

Lymph nodes of axilla

Lymphatic system

Arm

Elbow

Hip

Fallopian tube/Vas deferens

REFLEXES ON THE MEDIAL AND LATERAL SIDES OF THE RIGHT FOOT

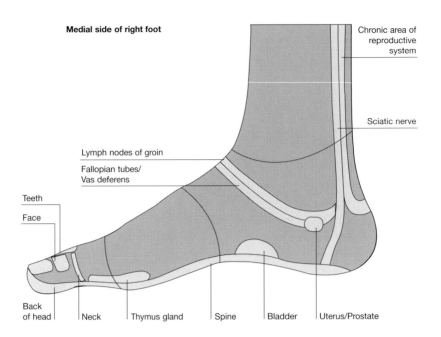

Medial side of right foot

Chronic area of reproductive system

Sciatic nerve

Lymph nodes of groin

Fallopian tubes/
Vas deferens

Teeth

Face

Back
of head | Neck | Thymus gland | Spine | Bladder | Uterus/Prostate

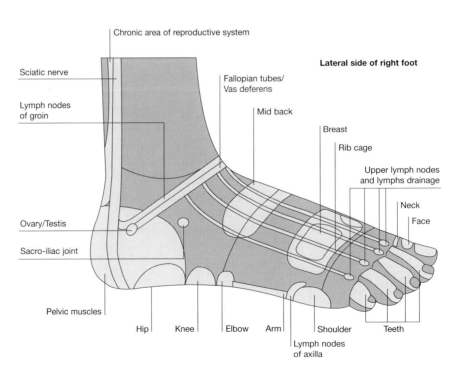

Chronic area of reproductive system

Sciatic nerve

Lymph nodes
of groin

Lateral side of right foot

Fallopian tubes/
Vas deferens

Mid back

Breast

Rib cage

Upper lymph nodes
and lymphs drainage

Neck

Face

Ovary/Testis

Sacro-iliac joint

Pelvic muscles |

Hip | Knee | Elbow | Arm | Shoulder | Teeth

Lymph nodes
of axilla

REFLEXES ON THE MEDIAL AND LATERAL SIDES OF THE LEFT FOOT

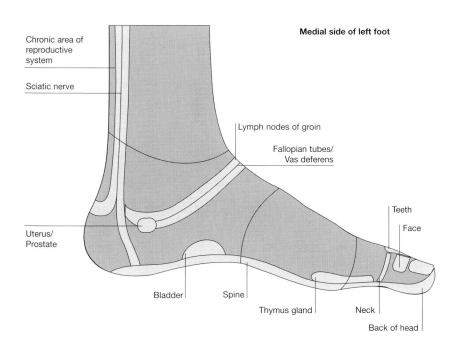

Medial side of left foot

Chronic area of reproductive system

Sciatic nerve

Lymph nodes of groin

Fallopian tubes/ Vas deferens

Teeth

Face

Uterus/ Prostate

Bladder

Spine

Thymus gland

Neck

Back of head

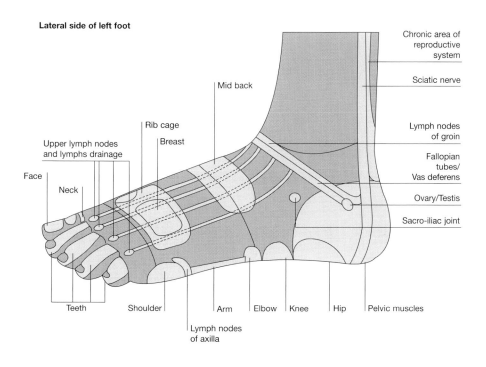

Lateral side of left foot

Chronic area of reproductive system

Sciatic nerve

Lymph nodes of groin

Fallopian tubes/ Vas deferens

Ovary/Testis

Sacro-iliac joint

Mid back

Rib cage

Breast

Upper lymph nodes and lymphs drainage

Face

Neck

Teeth

Shoulder

Arm

Elbow

Knee

Hip

Pelvic muscles

Lymph nodes of axilla

REFLEXES ON THE PALMS OF THE HANDS

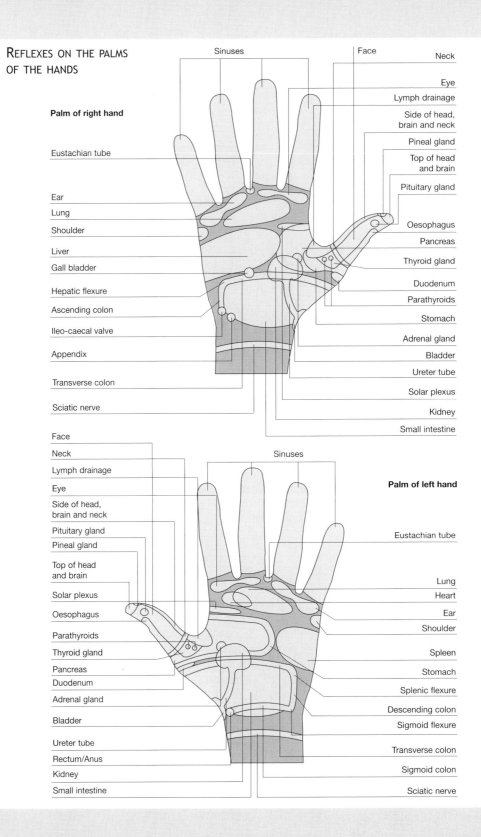

Palm of right hand

Eustachian tube

Ear
Lung
Shoulder
Liver
Gall bladder
Hepatic flexure
Ascending colon
Ileo-caecal valve
Appendix
Transverse colon
Sciatic nerve

Sinuses

Face
Neck
Eye
Lymph drainage
Side of head, brain and neck
Pineal gland
Top of head and brain
Pituitary gland
Oesophagus
Pancreas
Thyroid gland
Duodenum
Parathyroids
Stomach
Adrenal gland
Bladder
Ureter tube
Solar plexus
Kidney
Small intestine

Face
Neck
Lymph drainage
Eye
Side of head, brain and neck
Pituitary gland
Pineal gland
Top of head and brain
Solar plexus
Oesophagus
Parathyroids
Thyroid gland
Pancreas
Duodenum
Adrenal gland
Bladder
Ureter tube
Rectum/Anus
Kidney
Small intestine

Sinuses

Palm of left hand

Eustachian tube

Lung
Heart
Ear
Shoulder
Spleen
Stomach
Splenic flexure
Descending colon
Sigmoid flexure
Transverse colon
Sigmoid colon
Sciatic nerve

REFLEXES ON THE BACKS OF THE HANDS

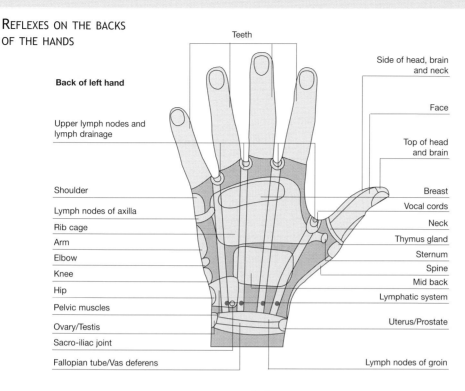

Back of left hand

Teeth

Upper lymph nodes and lymph drainage

Side of head, brain and neck

Face

Top of head and brain

Shoulder

Lymph nodes of axilla

Rib cage

Arm

Elbow

Knee

Hip

Pelvic muscles

Ovary/Testis

Sacro-iliac joint

Fallopian tube/Vas deferens

Breast

Vocal cords

Neck

Thymus gland

Sternum

Spine

Mid back

Lymphatic system

Uterus/Prostate

Lymph nodes of groin

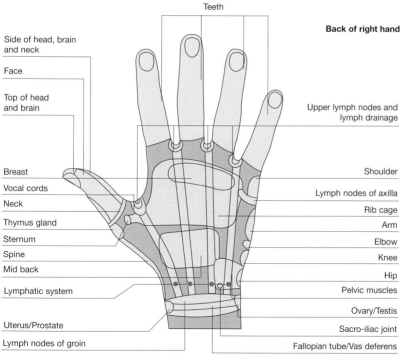

Teeth

Back of right hand

Side of head, brain and neck

Face

Top of head and brain

Upper lymph nodes and lymph drainage

Breast

Vocal cords

Neck

Thymus gland

Sternum

Spine

Mid back

Lymphatic system

Uterus/Prostate

Lymph nodes of groin

Shoulder

Lymph nodes of axilla

Rib cage

Arm

Elbow

Knee

Hip

Pelvic muscles

Ovary/Testis

Sacro-iliac joint

Fallopian tube/Vas deferens

The Spinal Column

The spinal column measures about 70 centimetres/28 inches in length in an average male, and about 60 centimetres/24 inches in an average female.

From the spinal cord come thirty-one pairs of spinal nerves. There are eight pairs of cervical, twelve pairs of thoracic, five pairs of lumbar, five pairs of sacral and one pair of coccygeal nerves. The individual nerves which arise from certain regions of the spinal cord join together to form a plexus.

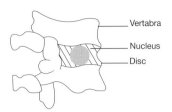

AN INTERVERTEBRAL DISC

Two plexuses are formed by the cervical nerves and one by the lumbar and sacral nerves. From these plexuses emerge individual peripheral nerves which serve different parts of the body. If there is a problem in a particular part of the body, it can be beneficial to work with the part of the spinal reflex which relates to the nerves that serve the problem area.

The spine comprises seven cervical, twelve thoracic, five lumbar, five sacral and four coccygeal vertebrae. The five sacral vertebrae are fused into one bone called the sacrum and the coccygeal vertebrae are fused into one or two bones called the coccyx.

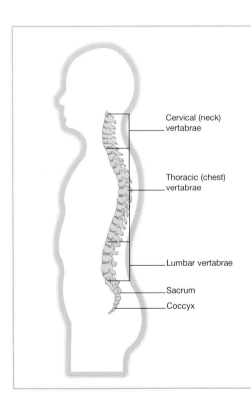

The human spine

The spinal column could be described as a strong flexible rod that moves anteriorly and laterally, and also rotates. It encloses and protects the spinal cord, supports the head and serves as a point of attachment for the ribs and muscles of the back. Between each vertebra are openings called intervertebral foramina, through which pass the nerves that connect the spinal cord to various parts of the body.

Between adjacent vertebrae, starting with the first vertebra in the neck and continuing to the sacrum, are fibrocartilaginous intervertebral discs. Each disc is composed of an outer fibrous ring consisting of fibrocartilage, and an inner, soft, pulpy elastic structure. These discs form strong joints and allow various movements of the vertebral column. They also absorb shock. Under compression they flatten, broaden and bulge from their intervertebral spaces.

Dowsing the spine

Using a diagram of the spinal column such as the one opposite, you may ask a patient to write his or her signature along the back of the spine; this acts as a witness for dowsing (see pages 48–49 for notes on dowsing). Dowse the spinal diagram to see if any of the vertebrae and their associated nerves are out of balance. When dowsing, always start from the top, the cervical spine, and work down to the coccyx. Where you discover imbalances, mark the vertebrae with a circle or cross. When you have finished, refer to the chart overleaf to see which part of the body is served by the nerves radiating from the imbalanced vertebrae. Now check the reflexes connected to these parts of the body to discover if there are any imbalances. These will show up as pain when the reflexes are worked, or the reflexes will feel very gritty. Treating these reflexes will allow prana to flow freely again.

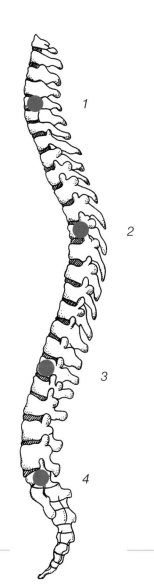

Example of a dowsed spine

Working down from the head on the diagram above:

1st imbalance is found in the 5th cervical vertebra. The nerves from this vertebra go to the vocal chords, neck glands and pharynx. Check these reflexes on the feet for energy stagnation or blockages.

2nd imbalance is found at the 6th thoracic vertebra. The nerves from this vertebra go to the stomach. Check the stomach reflex for energy stagnation.

3rd imbalance is sited at the 1st lumbar vertebra. The nerves go from here to the colon and inguinal rings. Check the colon reflex on both feet for blocked energy.

4th imbalance lies at the top of the sacrum. The nerves from here go to the hip bones and the buttocks. Check these reflexes, especially the sciatic loop.

  Points where imbalances are found.

The nerves connected to the spine

Nerve	Innervation	Some Related Conditions
1st Cervical	Blood supply to the head, pituitary, scalp, facial bones, brain, inner and middle ear, sympathetic nervous system	Headaches, nervousness, insomnia, head colds, hypertension, migraine, mental conditions, amnesia, epilepsy, tiredness, dizziness
2nd Cervical	Eyes, optic nerve, auditory nerve, sinuses, mastoid bones, tongue, forehead	Sinusitis, allergies, squint, deafness, eye troubles, earache, fainting spells, certain cases of blindness
3rd Cervical	Cheeks, outer ear, face bones, teeth, trifacial nerve	Neuralgia, neuritis, acne or pimples, eczema
4th Cervical	Nose, lips, mouth, eustachian tube, adenoids	Hay fever, catarrh, deafness, adenoid enlargement
5th Cervical	Vocal cords, neck glands, pharynx	Laryngitis, hoarseness, pharyngitis, quinsy
6th Cervical	Neck muscles, shoulders, tonsils	Stiff neck, pain in upper arm, croup, tonsillitis, whooping cough
7th Cervical	Thyroid gland, bursa in the shoulder, elbows	Bursitis, colds, thyroid conditions, goitre
1st Thoracic	Oesophagus and trachea, forearms, hands, wrists and fingers	Asthma, cough, difficult breathing, shortness of breath, pain in forearms and hands
2nd Thoracic	Heart, including its valves and covering, coronary arteries	Functional heart conditions and certain chest pains
3rd Thoracic	Lungs, bronchial tubes, pleura, chest, breast, nipples	Bronchitis, pleurisy, congestion, pneumonia, influenza
4th Thoracic	Gall bladder and common bile duct	Gall bladder conditions, jaundice, shingles
5th Thoracic	Liver, solar plexus, blood	Liver conditions, fevers, low blood pressure, anaemia, poor circulation, arthritis
6th Thoracic	Stomach	Stomach troubles, including nervous stomach, indigestion, heart burn, dyspepsia, etc.

Nerve	Innervation	Some Related Conditions
7th Thoracic	Pancreas, islets of langerhans, duodenum	Diabetes, ulcers, gastritis
8th Thoracic	Spleen, diaphragm	Leukaemia, hiccoughs, lowered resistance
9th Thoracic	Adrenals	Allergies, hives
10th Thoracic	Kidneys	Kidney problems, arteriosclerosis, chronic tiredness, nephritis, pyelitis
11th Thoracic	Kidneys, urethras	Skin conditions such as acne or pimples, eczema, boils etc., auto-intoxication
12th Thoracic	Small intestine, fallopian tubes, lymph circulation	Rheumatism, gas pains, certain types of sterility
1st Lumbar	Colon, inguinal rings	Constipation, colitis, dysentery, hernia, diarrhoea
2nd Lumbar	Appendix, abdomen, thighs, caecum	Appendicitis, cramps, difficult breathing, acidosis, varicose veins
3rd Lumbar	Sex organs, ovaries or testicles, uterus, bladder, knee	Menstrual problems such as painful or irregular periods, miscarriages, impotence, menopause, bladder problems, bed-wetting, knee pains
4th Lumbar	Prostate gland, muscles of lower back, sciatic nerve	Sciatica, lumbago, difficult, painful or too frequent urination
5th Lumbar	Legs, ankles, feet, heels, arches	Poor circulation, weakness and cramps of the lower extremities, swollen ankles and arches, cold feet
The Sacrum	Hip bones, buttocks	Sacro-iliac conditions, spinal curvature
The Coccyx	Rectum, anus	Haemorrhoids, itching, pain at end of spine on sitting

The Function of the Spine in Esoteric Teachings

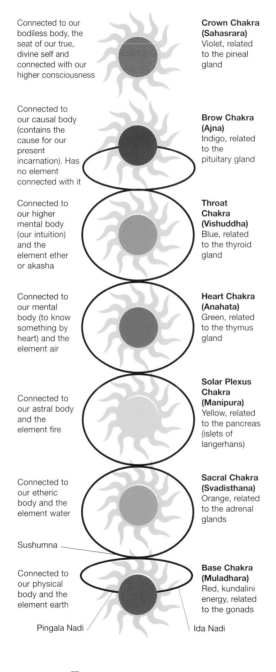

Connected to our bodiless body, the seat of our true, divine self and connected with our higher consciousness

Crown Chakra (Sahasrara)
Violet, related to the pineal gland

Connected to our causal body (contains the cause for our present incarnation). Has no element connected with it

Brow Chakra (Ajna)
Indigo, related to the pituitary gland

Connected to our higher mental body (our intuition) and the element ether or akasha

Throat Chakra (Vishuddha)
Blue, related to the thyroid gland

Connected to our mental body (to know something by heart) and the element air

Heart Chakra (Anahata)
Green, related to the thymus gland

Connected to our astral body and the element fire

Solar Plexus Chakra (Manipura)
Yellow, related to the pancreas (islets of langerhans)

Connected to our etheric body and the element water

Sacral Chakra (Svadisthana)
Orange, related to the adrenal glands

Sushumna

Connected to our physical body and the element earth

Base Chakra (Muladhara)
Red, kundalini energy, related to the gonads

Pingala Nadi

Ida Nadi

THE THREE MAIN NADIS AND THEIR PASSAGE ROUND THE CHAKRAS

In esoteric teachings the spine is regarded as very important. Humans are the only creatures, as far as we know, who stand and walk completely upright, carrying the spine in the vertical position. Most animals carry their spine in the horizontal position.

The spine in humankind has been referred to as a 'Jacob's ladder' which we climb in order to reach higher states of consciousness. It has been likened to a golden shaft of light which allows us to connect with both earth and spiritual energies and to experience heightened states of awareness.

Esoteric science teaches that our spinal column houses a threefold thread, commonly known as the three main *nadis*. In Eastern terminology these three *nadis* are called the *ida*, the *pingala* and the *sushumna* and are channels for the passage of three fire energies – electric fire, solar fire and fire by friction.

The *sushumna nadi* is situated inside the spinal column: it is the main channel for the flow of nervous energy and for these three fires. The *sushumna* extends from the base chakra to the brow chakra, passing through the four major chakras situated between them. In the *sushumna* are two additional *nadis*, *vajra* and *chitrini*: these are enclosed within one another, and it is the 'tube' within the finest of these that is the conduit for the *kundalini* energy. This energy is the union of the three fires, and when the seven main chakras or energy centres are open and a person is ready mentally, physically and spiritually, *kundalini* energy rises through the *sushumna* to the crown chakra to bring about a state of enlightenment, *samadhi*, nirvana or God consciousness.

The *ida nadi* is situated on the left side of our body and the *pingala* on the right. Both extend from the base chakra, intertwining the major chakras and the *sushumna* in a serpentine pattern to their point of termination, the brow chakra. *Ida* is associated with coolness, the moon, the right hemisphere of the brain and the parasympathetic nervous system. *Pingala* is linked with the sun, heat, the left hemisphere of the brain and the sympathetic nervous system. *Ida* and *pingala* receive their supply of prana through the process of respiration and are connected to the left and right nostril respectively.

The spinal column with its esoteric counterpart is primarily intended to be the channel through which the energizing of the chakras and the distribution of energy to the surrounding areas of the body takes place. Failure of this function causes energy imbalances and blockages which manifest as disease in the physical body.

The metamorphic technique

The metamorphic technique, discovered by Robert St John, bases treatment on the spinal reflex found on the feet, hands and head. Robert St

John believes that it is in the nine-month gestation period that the potentials of an individual's life are established. He finds that working on the spinal reflexes brings pre-natal experiences back into focus and the life force of the individual can then release any energies that were impeded during that period. The healing process of body, mind and spirit is thus allowed to take place.

He has divided the spinal reflex on the feet and hands into six sections. The first section is found on the first and second phalanges of the big toe. This is prior to the spinal reflex and represents pre-conception. The second section is situated at the first cervical vertebra and stands for conception. The third section extends from the first to the tenth thoracic vertebrae and is post-conception (1–22 weeks). The fourth section, quickening (18–22 weeks), lies between the eighth and tenth thoracic vertebrae. The fifth section, pre-birth (18–38 weeks), is found between the tenth thoracic vertebra and and the coccyx, and the sixth section, birth, is located at the coccyx.

In *The Metamorphic Technique* by Gaston St Pierre and Debbie Boater, it is suggested that this form of treatment should be given to a complete family unit as opposed to a single individual. Metamorphic treatment can precipitate such dramatic changes in an individual that an untreated family can find it difficult to understand and cope with the situation.

The History of Colour Therapy
Its earliest beginnings

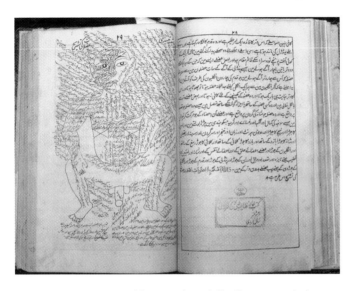

AYURVEDIC TEXTBOOK.

Many ancient civilizations regarded colour as a manifestation of the life-giving light and for this reason they related it to their deities. Athena, the daughter of Zeus, is reported to have worn a golden robe; to Ceres, the Roman goddess of nature, the red poppy was sacred; and the colour worn by the Buddha was either yellow or gold. In Brahmanism, yellow is a sacred colour, and in the Upanishads (a sacred Hindu scripture) it is written: 'In the supreme golden chamber is Brahman, invisible and pure. He is the radiant light of all lights.' Judaism's holy colours are red, blue, purple and white and the sacred colour of Mohammed is green.

Healing temples

The use of colour as a vibrational therapy goes back many centuries. According to Frank Alper in his book *Exploring Atlantis*, the Atlanteans used light and colour not only to treat physical disease but to heal relationships, to assist childbirth and to aid the dying in their transition from earthly to spiritual life. They built temples, described by Frank Alper in his book as being circular with a domed roof constructed from interlocking crystals. These crystals refracted the sunlight, filling the temple with the spectral colours. Around the circumference of the temple were individual healing rooms with doors said to resonate to the required colour frequencies. Archaeologists have discovered that the Egyptian healing temples were similarly constructed.

Egyptian deities

The two most important healing divinities of the ancient Egyptians were Thoth and Imhotep. To Thoth, patron god of physicians and scribes, the use of colour in healing was attributed. Thoth, in his incarnation as Hermes Trismegistus, applied colour through herbs and plants, salves and dyes, and through coloured minerals and metals such as copper, carbon and antimony. Antimony, thought to have antiseptic properties, was used in Egyptian eye make-up, maybe to prevent eye disease.

Indian traditions

India is a country alive with colour and has always utilized this in its healing practices. Its Ayurvedic medicine is founded upon ancient Vedic wisdom. Traditionally, diagnosis has used magical as well as intellectual approaches. Treatment has included the use of minerals and gemstones, which were believed to be a concentration of the cosmic rays. Onyx was related to ultra violet light, cat's-eye to infra-red, ruby to red, pearl to orange, coral to yellow, emerald to green, topaz to blue, diamond to indigo and sapphire to violet.

Ancient Chinese medicine

Classical Chinese medicine is based on the great medical compendium the *Nei Ching* (Canon of Medicine) compiled by Y Hsiung, the Yellow Emperor. According to the *Nei Ching*, there were five methods of treatment; cure the spirit, nourish the body, give medication, treat the whole body and use acupuncture and moxibustion. Colour was applied in the form of herbs, minerals and salves. Scientist Peter Mandel has recently re-introduced colour to this ancient art of healing in the form of 'colourpuncture'. Mandel discovered that focusing coloured light on acupuncture points triggered powerful healing impulses in the physical and energy bodies, so his technique involves administering the appropriate colours to those points needing treatment.

Greek and Roman practices

A common practice amongst the Greeks and Romans was treatment by sunlight (heliotherapy), which Herodotus is supposed to have introduced. The famous healing temples in the Greek city of Heliopolis were designed to refract sunlight into its spectral colours using methods similar to those of the Atlantean and Egyptian temples.

In ancient Greece, also, is found a healing system attributed to Pythagoras, who established there a philosophical medical centre based on Orphic mysticism. Here students worked with the science of numbers, establishing scientific theories of sound and of musical octaves which they used for healing in conjunction with colour.

Hippocrates

Hippocrates, a Greek physician often said to be the father of modern medicine, is rumoured to have worked with the Greek system which explained illness in terms of four basic humours or bodily fluids. It was believed that when these humours were kept in equilibrium, harmony and health were established. Hippocrates was known to be an Alchemist and to employ both colour and magic in his healing techniques: these would have included the use of flowers, plasters, ointments and minerals. His most widely known medical text, containing both affirmations and prohibitions, is the Hippocratic Oath.

BUST OF HIPPOCRATES (460–370 BC).

The History of Colour Therapy
From the first century AD

The early Christian church tended to equate disease with punishment for sin, and healing with grace and divine intervention, deeming pagan those medical practices involving colour, chants and worship of gods other than its own. This drove such practices underground, where the ancient knowledge was passed on orally. Unfortunately, many Greek and Roman writings on holistic medical procedures were lost. What medical scripts remained were preserved and translated, first into Arabic and later

ENGRAVING OF THE PERSIAN PHYSCIAN AND PHILOSOPHER AVICENNA.

into Latin, by the evangelical religion of Islam, the most frequently translated works being those of Aristotle, Hippocrates and the Greek physician Galen.

Colour was restored to medical practices by the outstanding Persian physician Avicenna (980–circa 1037), reputedly the writer of 100 books, the most renowned being *The Canon* in which he referred to his own research into the use of colour treatments. He used mainly red, blue and yellow, claiming that yellow reduced inflammation and pain, red increased blood pressure and blue lowered it. Interestingly, he was also the first to voice the adverse effects that colour can produce.

Throughout the Middle Ages and Renaissance, medical treatment was derived from the re-definition of the classical conception of humours, administering colour through plant extracts and salves. An outstanding Renaissance healer, born in Zurich, was Theophrastus Bombastus von Hohenkeim, known as Paracelsus. He had a doctor's degree, and a deep interest in alchemy which led him to administer healing colour through light, as well as through herbs and minerals.

The nineteenth century

By the nineteenth century, the dissection of corpses had led to great advances in the understanding of anatomy, and the use of drugs was growing. Gradually, the concept of treating the whole person was lost, emphasis being placed on diseases of the physical body. With the exclusion of the spiritual, emotional and mental aspects, colour fell into disuse. Its re-emergence during the nineteenth century was attributed to Dr Seth Pancoast and Dr Edwin Babitt.

Pancoast's interest lay in the Kabala and the wisdom of ancient philosophers: upon these teachings some of his colour-related knowledge was based. In 1897 he published *Blue and Red Lights*, in which he describes his use of blue and red filters in treatment. He believed that the blue rays relaxed the nervous system and red rays accelerated it. One year later, Babitt published *The Principles of Light and Colour*. His theory, based on the three primary colours of red, yellow and blue, suggested that yellow was the colour of luminosity, red was the colour of heat and blue was associated with electricity. He invented machines for administering colours to his patients and gave them water solarised with an appropriate colour to drink.

The twentieth century

At the beginning of the twentieth century, colour was being investigated by the occultist, philosopher, teacher and religious leader Rudolf Steiner. He considered colour to be a living entity (each colour bearing a spiritual significance) destined to play a vital role in twenty-first-century medicine. He worked primarily with red, blue and yellow (naming them 'active colours') and green, white, black and peach blossom (calling them 'image colours'). He related colour to mathematical form, believing that form had the power to amplify colour's effect.

Two great twentieth-century pioneers of colour therapy were Dinsaha P Ghadiali and Dr Harry Spitler. Ghadiali, a qualified physicist, formulated a scientific approach for the application of colour, relating the specific vibrational energies of twelve colours to human physiology and transmitting the appropriate colour to his patient through one of the two machines he invented. In 1934 he published his three-volume work *The Spectro-Chrome Metry Encyclopaedia* which constituted a home colour-training course. He had no medical training, but was awarded four honorary medical degrees for his research into colour.

Spitler, a doctor and optometrist, originated a system of colour treatment called syntonics, which applied light directly through the eyes. Using syntonics on animals convinced Spitler that light entering the eyes played an important role in the functioning of both the endocrine system and the autonomic nervous system. He concluded that syntonics was able to change a person's vision due to the eyes' dependence on the nervous system.

In 1977, Jacob Liberman, an American optometrist, heard of Spitler's work, attended one of his courses and carried on where Spitler had left off. Subsequently, Liberman pioneered a therapeutic light treatment which he called 'ocular phototherapy'. He has published two books on his work: *Light: Medicine of the Future* and *Take Off Your Glasses and See*. As beings of light, Liberman says, our eyes radiate the light contained within us, and we need light to maintain our well-being.

Treatment with Sunlight

Sunlight treatment involves the absorption of the full colour spectrum present in sunlight. I must remind the reader here that to sit in sunlight for extended periods of time is dangerous especially considering current reports on the disintegration of parts of the ozone layer. Equally dangerous is looking directly at the sun: this can cause serious damage to the eyes.

As I have already mentioned, treatment by sunlight (heliotherapy) was a common practice among the Greeks and Romans but, with the

advent of Christianity, the practice continued in secret. It was re-introduced towards the middle of the nineteenth century by Jakob Lorber author of *The Healing Power of Sunlight*, published in 1851 in Germany. Maintaining that the information contained in his book came directly from God, Lorber advocated that any part of the body suffering disease should be exposed to the sun's rays. He also emphasized the importance of appropriate diet and the drinking of clear, clean, sun-infiltrated spring water. Lorber treated his patients with solarised saclose tablets and with solarised pure sea salt,

THE UPLIFTING POWER OF SUNLIGHT.
We have more energy when the sun shines and less on a dull, overcast day.

considering the latter to be a good remedy for bone fractures. He believed that solarised salt placed on the tongue of those near to death would completely restore them, provided that they were not too emaciated. Another of his practices was to solarise the blood from a healthy lamb or calf until the blood turned into a reddish brown powder. This he recommended as a remedy for lung disease and haemorrhage.

Heliotherapy and science

Another pioneer of sunlight treatment, and the first to develop it scientifically, was the Danish physician Niels Ryberg Finsen (1860–1904). He used artificial light, through the instrument known as the carbon arc, to treat skin tuberculosis (*lupus vulgaris*). Having observed that this disease was more prevalent in winter, he deduced that sunlight played an important role in curing it. For his many years of work in this field he received, in 1903, the Nobel Prize and became known as the Father of Photobiology.

The most acclaimed person for using heliotherapy on a large scale was Dr Augustus Rollier. Rollier used it in his Swiss sanatoria for the treatment and prevention of tuberculosis. When he first presented evidence of his cures at a medical congress in Paris, the audience ridiculed him. Undeterred, he continued his work, setting up thirty-six treatment clinics. He believed in the healing power of the sun and, to support his claim, took photographs of patients before and after treatment.

Another pioneer, John Ott, worked to prove the essentiality of ultra violet light for our health. Ott was a banker by profession and worked with time-lapse photography as a hobby. Through controlled experiments with mice and plants, he discovered that those living in natural daylight survived for longer than those living under artificial light, which eliminates the ultra violet ray. Ott himself suffered from arthritis. One day he broke his glasses and had no option but to spend some time pursuing his outdoor work without them. He subsequently discovered an improvement in his arthritic condition. This fact, together with the results of later experiments, led him to believe that full spectrum light absorbed through the eyes is essential for health.

At this present time the medical profession is using various forms of light treatment. Studies carried out in the 1960s suggested that blue light was able to rid jaundiced babies' bodies of the bilirubin that the immature liver was unable to cope with (J R Lacy, *Neonatal Jaundice & Phototherapy*).

A condition that is being treated with full spectrum light is Seasonal Affective Disorder (SAD). This condition, discovered by Dr Norman Rosenthal, himself a sufferer, starts with the onset of autumn and disappears in the spring. It is caused by high levels in the blood, during daylight hours, of the hormone melatonin. The presenting symptoms are lethargy, depression and a craving for carbohydrates. This condition can be treated by sitting in front of a SAD light box. This light box houses up to six full-spectrum, flicker-free, fluorescent tubes. The length of time needed to absorb sufficient light through one's eyes depends upon the strength of the light the box emits.

More Recent Use of Light

Lasers

Treatment with lasers (Light Amplification by Stimulated Emission of Radiation) is one fairly recent use of light. Unlike the light given off by atoms, laser light is of a single wavelength, all the waves being in phase with each other or 'coherent'. This allows a very high level of energy to be projected as a parallel beam. The great advantages of lasers are their potency, their speed of action and their ability to focus on a minute area, allowing great advances to be made in microsurgery, particularly fibreoptic endoscopy.

Lasers have two main uses in surgery: for endoscopic photocoagulation of bleeding vessels, using the visible green wavelength produced by the argon laser; for the incision of tissue, using the infra-red beam of the carbon dioxide laser. Lasers can remove small benign tumours such as verrucas, can obliterate 'port wine stains' and remove tattoos. They also play an important role in ophthalmology, in the treatment of detached retinas and of proliferative retinopathy (a condition associated with diabetes). Fairly recently, lasers have been used for tonsillectomies, advantageously reducing the haemorrhaging often associated with the operation.

A treatment pioneered by Professor Mester at Semmelweis University, Budapest, is the use of soft laser light for the amelioration of burn victims' pain and the acceleration of wound healing. Another treatment, developed in Budapest by Dr Marta Fenyo, a biophysicist, laser specialist and inventor, uses polarized light. Initially she worked alongside Professor Mester, researching the effects of soft lasers on leg ulcers, bed sores and varicose problems. But, lacking the funds to purchase the equipment necessary to treat sufferers, she instead began researching the component in laser light responsible for healing these conditions, and discovered polarized light.

Whilst researching polarized light, she met Dr Fritz Hollwich. Hollwich's research centred upon people's biological response to fluorescent light and full spectrum light and upon Professor Blackwell's research into polarized artificial light. Hollwich and Fenyo discovered that polarized light boosts the immune system and has a dramatic healing effect on varicose ulcers. Using polarized light, Fenyo treated mice infected with cancerous tumours. She found that their life expectancy increased, sometimes up to a full-life span. From dogs dying of cancer she extracted a tiny portion of blood, treated it with polarized light and then re-infused it, producing significant tumour shrinkage.

Other research into light therapy

Several other forms of light treatment are presently being used by the medical profession. In Russia, Professor Kira Samoilova is working with ultra-violet irradiated blood retransfusions (UVIBR) and intravenous visible laser light irradiation of blood (ILIB), developed in the mid 1980s.

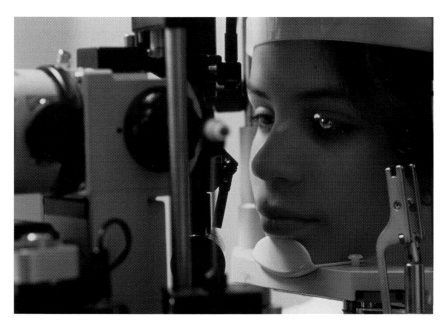

LASER EYE SURGERY.
The surgeon aims the laser using a retinal camera.
The laser is delivered in a series of pulses.

Samoilova's work furthers that of Dr Emmit Knott and Dr Virgil Hancock. In 1934, Knott and Hancock published their findings concerning the use of Knott's invention – the Haemo-Irradiation Machine. The purpose of this was to irradiate with ultra-violet light a small amount of the patient's blood. With this UVIBR therapy they successfully treated viral infections, peritonitis and advanced toxaemia, discovering that UVIBR worked where drug treatment had failed.

In 1970 photodynamic therapy (PDT), a new treatment using red light, was pioneered by American Research chemist Dr Thomas Dougherty (see 'Photoradiation Therapy – new approaches', Seminars in Surgical Oncology 6–16 and 'Photosensitization of Malignant Tumours' in S Ecomon, Lea & Febinger, 1980). He discovered that when porphyrins, light-sensitive complex organic compounds forming the basis of respiratory pigments (for example haemoglobin and myoglobin), were injected into the blood stream,

they were eliminated from all but malignant cells. When the patient was then subjected to ultra-violet light, the malignant tumours 'lit up'. Illumination of these tumours with red caused the tumours to die.

A recent development in Britain is 'interstitial PDT'. Developed from the research of Professor Stanley Brown, it is used with large and deep-seated tumours. Professor Brown has also applied red light around the site where a malignant tumour has been removed, to eliminate any remaining cancer cells. PDT is also being used on skin cancers.

Learning about the latest research on light therapy has led me to believe that treatment with all aspects of light, which includes colour, will be the medicine of the future. Perhaps the only necessary item in a future first aid kit will be a soft laser. A wonderful thought!

Light and Colour

In 1666 a university student, Isaac Newton, became fascinated by experiments on light carried out by a French scientist, Rene Descartes. Descartes, noting how a prism could split white light into the spectrum colours, had assumed that the varying thickness of the prism was responsible for this phenomenon. Newton tested Descartes' theory by designing a simple experiment of his own, concluding from it that white light actually contained the different colours, the prism revealing rather than producing them. When light entered the prism it was refracted due to its speed being altered: this refraction accounted for the appearance of the colours because each colour has a different angle of refraction. When we see a rainbow appearing with the sun after a storm, the raindrops are acting like prisms, refracting the sun's light.

The colours we see, together with other, invisible, electromagnetic rays, form the electromagnetic spectrum. All electromagnetic energy originates from the sun and ranges from the longest wavelengths (radio waves) to the shortest (cosmic rays).

Considering the properties, and the scientific and medical uses of the invisible rays on this spectrum poses for me an interesting question. If medicine and other sciences concede that the invisible part of the spectrum affects human beings, how can it then be maintained that the wavelengths and frequencies of the visible part do not? Through my work with colour and light, I have come to believe that they affect us, as beings of light, greatly.

THE REFRACTION OF LIGHT THROUGH A PRISM.

The electromagnetic spectrum

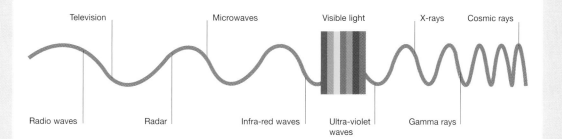

Television Microwaves Visible light X-rays Cosmic rays

Radio waves Radar Infra-red waves Ultra-violet waves Gamma rays

The longest waves – radio waves – are used for broadcasting and communicating systems, including radio, television and radar. Industry uses them to raise the temperature of metals for hardening purposes.

The short-wave bands are used for distance broadcasting and also for diathermy, where electric currents are applied to produce heat in the deeper tissues of the body for the relief of rheumatism, arthritis and neuralgia.

Microwave radiation, used in ovens, rapidly changes the alignment of water molecules to heat the food.

Infra-red waves are produced by anything that is hot. They include photographic and radiant heat waves and have the power to travel great distances and penetrate heavy atmospheres. Photographic plates are sensitive to them, and so they can be used to take pictures of objects difficult for the human eye to see. Radiant heat waves are used in electric heaters and infrared lamps.

Following infra-red comes visible light. This part of the electromagnetic spectrum can be seen by our eyes because the nerve endings (called rods and cones) are sensitive to this particular range of wavelengths. The rods are responsible for night vision and the cones for distinguishing the colours of light.

From visible light we pass to the invisible rays of ultra-violet waves. Under ultra-violet certain substances become luminous; for example, butter glows yellow, margarine glows blue, and cancer tissue glows a vivid

yellow. The longest ultra-violet rays produce fluorescent light which, though widely used, has been shown to be detrimental to health. The shorter erythemal rays are responsible for producing a suntan and are used in the synthetic production of vitamin D.

As the wavelengths become shorter, we come to x-rays. These include soft x-rays (grenz rays) and hard x-rays. Hard x-rays can destroy body cells and are used to treat malignant tumours. They are used medically for deep-seated afflictions and by industry to detect metal flaws. Soft x-rays, which do minimal damage, are used for x-raying the physical body, and are invaluable to the medical profession for diagnostic purposes. Overdoses, though, can cause serious damage – anaemia, roentgen sickness, carcinomas and, if used during pregnancy, foetal deformities.

Further down the scale are the gamma or radium rays. Highly dangerous if not carefully monitored, they were discovered by Pierre and Marie Curie early in the twentieth century. These are specially penetrating rays, emitted by a radioactive substance such as radium and are used mainly in the treatment of cancerous tumours.

Cosmic rays, with the shortest wavelengths, have the highest energy radiation. They contain tiny particles of atomic nuclei, as well as some electrons and gamma rays. Cosmic radiation bombards the earth's atmosphere from remote regions of space.

The Aura

The aura surrounding each person is that individual's unique electromagnetic field. Through the techniques of Kirlian photography (a high frequency photograph named after its inventors Semyon and Valentina Kirlian) and PIP imaging, the work of Harry Oldfield (see Harry Oldfield's *Invisible Universe*), the aura can be captured on photographs.

The aura is ovoid in shape, being widest at the head and the most narrow at the feet. It is a living part of us that is constantly expanding and contracting with our incoming and outgoing thoughts and feelings. The full extent of the aura's expansion is entirely dependent upon a person's

THE NADIS FOUND IN THE ETHERIC BODY
(Taken from an ancient parchment.)

spiritual growth and awareness.

The aura comprises six layers or sheaths which interpenetrate each other and the physical body. Each layer has its own vibrational frequency and display of colours, which changes when there is disharmony within it or within any of the other layers. The degree to which a person is able to perceive the aura is dependent on the range of frequencies he or she is able to 'tune in' to.

The etheric body

The layer nearest the physical body is the etheric, sometimes known as the etheric double because it is the energetic blueprint of the physical body. The etheric layer underlies and permeates every part of the physical body, and extends for approximately 5 centimetres/2 inches beyond it.

The etheric is composed of millions of tiny energy channels, called *nadis*, through which prana flows. These weave the intricate etheric web that surrounds and permeates every form. While they appear as separate strands, in reality they form an interlocking cord known as the silver cord.

The *nadis* are closely linked with the physical body's nervous system. Where a number of *nadis* intersect, an energy centre or chakra is formed. The intersection of seven *nadis* forms an acupuncture point; fourteen *nadis* create a minor chakra and twenty-one a major chakra. Each major chakra is linked with a specific gland in the physical body.

The etheric body is controlled by thought: to bring it into its full functioning right and pure thinking is required. The etheric itself is never sick but what it does is absorb both internal and external conditions, which ultimately manifest as physical disease. The internal conditions arise from our emotional and mental states, the external conditions from our diet and lifestyle, and environmental factors.

The astral body

The second layer is the astral or emotional body. This interpenetrates both the physical and etheric but, because it is slightly larger, it extends beyond them for up to 30 centimetres /12 inches. The astral body has three general functions. These are: to make sensation possible; to serve as a bridge between the mind and the physical body; to act as an independent vehicle of consciousness and action.

A principle feature of the astral body is the variety of colours that constantly flows through it. These colours are an expression of our feelings and emotions. For example, deep red flashes, usually against a black background, symbolize anger. Pure, clear red is physical love; rose pink shows unselfish love. A clear orange is joy and optimism, but when this colour becomes dull and muddy it reflects pride and ambition. A dull, muddy green is envy, a clear blue expresses spiritual devotion and a bright, vivid grey is linked with fear.

The astral does slowly wear away and needs 'care and feeding'. To achieve this it attracts replacement particles from the surrounding astral environment. The astral body's health depends upon the quality of particles attracted. A good astral diet comes from constructive feelings, uplifting aspirations and selfless love.

The mental body

Larger than the astral body and composed of more refined matter is the aura's third layer, the mental body, whose development arises from constructive thoughts. It is said to be a body of great beauty because the rapid motion of its particles gives it an aspect of living iridescent light. This light becomes more radiant with the evolution of the intellect and an orientation towards spiritual concepts. Every thought creates in the mental body a vibration, which is accompanied by a play of vivid colour.

According to theosophical teaching, the mental body rotates rapidly on its axis, creating a series of coloured bands. These bands are said to be determined by our thoughts. In their book *Thought Forms*, Annie Besant and C W Leadbeater stress that every thought we entertain creates a shape or form, the broad band in the middle section of the mental body being devoted to these. Besant and Leadbeater explain how our thoughts can be projected into the atmosphere, to places and people, through visualization. They also emphasize that like attracts like: if we harbour negative thoughts, these will attract negative thoughts of a like nature, thereby amplifying the negativity. However, if we think positively we will attract to ourselves positive thoughts.

40

The higher mental body

Next to the mental body, and extending beyond it, lies the higher mental body. This body is related to our intuition. For practitioners of complementary therapies, the development of this layer is of prime importance. Although there are set colours for specific diseases, because each person is an individual this sometimes necessitates a different treatment colour from the norm. One way a practitioner can discover this variant colour is by using intuition.

The colours flowing through the higher mental body are dependent upon how open our intuition is and to what extent we are influenced by the mental body. In a person with evolved intuition this part of the aura is permeated by subtle shades of blue and violet.

The causal body

Next to the higher mental is the causal body which, together with the last

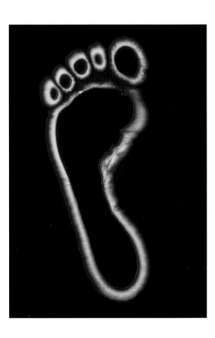

layer of the aura, is not yet fully developed in the majority of people. This makes the colours displayed there difficult to see by those few people who have the ability to access these more refined layers.

The causal body is so named because it is where, among other information, the cause for our present incarnation is stored. I believe that we re-incarnate in order to perform certain tasks, experience different situations and to pay back karma. (Karma is the law of cause and effect.) All our earthly experiences serve to aid our spiritual growth and development.

This layer of the aura houses information on all of an individual's past lives but, unless it is necessary for spiritual growth, the average person is unable to access these. It may be that we have enough to cope with in this present lifetime without trying to relive the traumas of the past.

The bodiless body

The last and largest layer of the aura is named the bodiless body. It represents our true self, our divinity, which has no beginning and no ending. It is the essence which knows all things and has chosen to incarnate into a physical body in order to experience certain earthly conditions.

Among these conditions is free will – the liberty to choose how we as individuals conduct our lives. Working with the other layers of the aura will finally lead us to experience the glory and divinity of this final layer – a practice which takes many lifetimes to accomplish.

KIRLIAN PHOTOGRAPH OF A HUMAN FOOT.
This photographic technique reveals the electromagnetic discharge around the foot's edge.

The Chakras

The word chakra is Sanskrit for 'a wheel' or 'circle'. These wheels are rotating energy centres located in the etheric layer of the aura but interacting with the physical body and the rest of the aura. There are seven major, twenty-one minor and one lesser-known major chakra, the alta major. According to David Tansley in *Radionics and the Subtle Bodies of Man* the seven major chakras are formed at points where the nadis cross twenty-one times. The twenty-one minor chakras are located at points where the nadis cross fourteen times.

The minor chakras

The twenty-one minor chakras are distributed thus: one in front of each ear; one behind each eye; one midway along each clavicle; one near the thymus gland; one behind the nipple of each breast; one in the palm of each hand; one near the liver; one connected with the stomach; two connected with the spleen; one related to each gonad; one behind each knee and one on the sole of each foot.

The major chakras

Five major chakras are situated in line with the spine. The first, the base chakra, is located at the perineum; the second, the sacral chakra, is located in the lower abdomen, centred between the navel and the genitals; the third, the solar plexus chakra, is found over the adrenal glands; the fourth, the heart chakra, relates to the cardiac plexus; the fifth, the throat chakra, is located in the neck region, between the two clavicle bones. The sixth chakra, the brow, is found at the

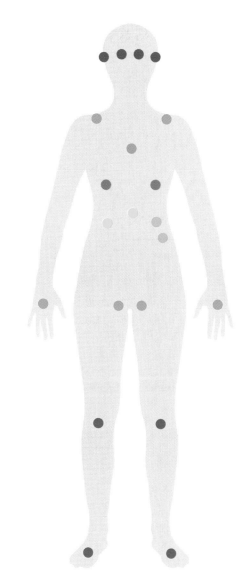

THE POSITION OF THE MINOR CHAKRAS

centre of the head, slightly above the eyes; the crown chakra, the seventh, is situated at the crown of the head; the alta major chakra, the eighth, is located at the medulla oblongata, sometimes referred to as the 'mouth of God' because here cosmic energy flows into the body.

The position of the chakras on the foot

Each of the first seven major chakras works with a specific endocrine gland and the eighth, the alta major, is connected with the carotid glands. Each chakra radiates one of the spectral colours. On a higher level they form a spiritual ladder leading to enlightenment.

Because, together, the feet are a mirror image of the whole body, the major chakras can be located along the spinal reflex on both left and right feet. The base chakra is situated towards the back of the calcaneus. The sacral chakra is where the calcaneus and navicular bones join. The solar plexus chakra is at the base of the metatarsal bone, while the heart chakra is located at its head. The throat chakra is found approximately midway along the second phalanges, in line with the base of the big toe. The brow chakra is found where the first and second phalanges meet, and the crown chakra is located on top of the big toe. The alta major chakra is at the base of the pad of the big toe, close to the spinal reflex.

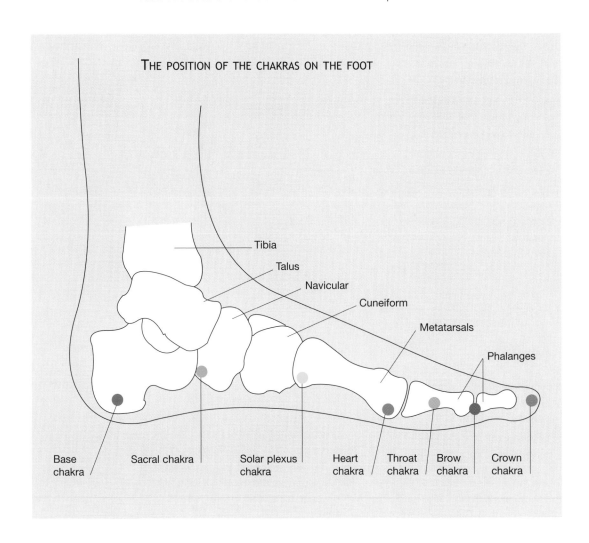

THE POSITION OF THE CHAKRAS ON THE FOOT

Tibia

Talus

Navicular

Cuneiform

Metatarsals

Phalanges

Base chakra

Sacral chakra

Solar plexus chakra

Heart chakra

Throat chakra

Brow chakra

Crown chakra

Treating the chakras

Treating the chakras is important. I have found, during my years of practice, one or more of them to be out of balance in the average person. Remembering, too, that the chakras are associated with specific glands, it is equally important to treat them in people suffering hormonal imbalances or endocrine gland problems.

My method is to give an initial reflexology treatment, then treat any painful reflexes with the appropriate colours. Next I treat the chakras and, finally, administer the overall colour.

To treat the chakras, I first dowse to see if the chakra is in balance (see pages 48–49 for notes on dowsing). If it is, I do not treat. If the chakra is out of balance, I dowse to discover if it is over- or under-active.

An over-active chakra contains too much of its own energy, so I apply the complementary colour to bring it into balance. An under-active chakra is treated with the colour it vibrates to – the general colour. Refer to the chart below and consult the individual colour chapters for further information on dowsing and treating the chakras.

THE POSITION OF THE MAJOR CHAKRAS

Chakra	General Colour	Complementary Colour
Base chakra		
Sacral chakra		
Solar plexus chakra		
Heart chakra		
Throat chakra		
Brow chakra		
Crown chakra		
Alta Major chakra	Magenta or white	Lime green or white

Colour

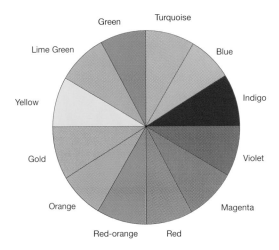

THE TWELVE-COLOUR WHEEL

ADDITIVE COLOUR

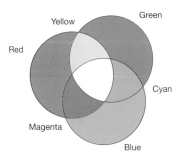

SUBTRACTIVE COLOUR

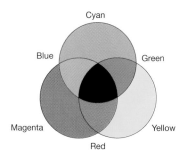

The colours nature surrounds us with and the colours we use in our clothes and décor have the power to lift or depress our spirits, to stimulate and tranquillize, to provoke and antagonize. These colours originate from either light or pigment.

Additive colour mixing

The process of mixing light is known as 'additive colour mixing' because the colour obtained is the result of combining, or adding colours together. In his experiments Isaac Newton used all the spectral colours to produce white light. However, later experiments have shown that only three of the additive primaries are needed – red, green and blue light. These primaries can be used in various combinations to produce almost any other colour.

Subtractive colour mixing

Mixing dyes or pigments or superimposing transparent coloured filters is called 'subtractive colour mixing'. This is because the colour obtained is the result of the simultaneous or successive subtraction of various colours from the light passing through the pigment or through the combination of filters.

When working with pigment or 'subtractive colour' white cannot be produced, for when the red, blue and green primaries are overlapped and subjected to white light, all three colours are taken from the light leaving black. When the three colours are added together in pairs, the secondary colours of cyan, yellow and magenta are formed.

The number of colours used in therapy varies with each practitioner. At the Oracle School of Colour we have chosen to work with twelve main colours plus rose pink, silver and pearl. We incorporate in our teaching the vibrational energies of sound, and our twelve main colours relate to the chromatic scale.

The characteristics of seven of the twelve colours are given in the chapters dealing with the colours relating to the physical body. Apart from lime green (which is covered in Green) descriptions of the remaining colours are given separately at the end of the book.

Complementary colour

When therapists work with colour we almost always use the required colour alongside its complementary. Complementary pairs of pigment colour are those which, when mixed together in the same proportion, produce grey. With coloured light, such a mixture would produce white. To find a colour's complementary, look diagonally across it on the colour wheel (see diagram opposite). For example, the complementary colour of red is green.

The complementary colour is used alongside the treatment colour because human beings are composed of opposites. We have a right and left hemisphere to our brain; if we breathe in we must breathe out; we contain both the male and female energies. In order to become whole, we have to accept these opposites and then transcend them. By using a colour together with its complementary we are working with opposites in order to help bring about a state of wholeness.

When working with colour therapy, many techniques can be employed. My own method utilizes colour in three ways through what I term the general colour, the treatment colour and the overall colour.

General colour

These are the colours to which specific parts of the physical body vibrate naturally and are, with a few exceptions, determined by the colour of the nearest major chakra. These colours are used on reflexes that are painful but have no associated physical disease. A reflex can be painful for three reasons. First, it can be associated with a physical disease. Secondly, there may be an accumulation of stagnant energy in the aura, overshadowing the part of the body that the painful reflex relates to. If this stagnant energy is ignored, it can eventually manifest as physical disease. The third reason for a reflex being painful is because the part of the body relating to it is compensating for disease and malfunction in another part of the body.

Treatment colour

This is the colour applied, with its complementary colour, to the reflex(es) associated with a physical disease.

Overall colour

This colour helps a person find and work with the cause of the disease. I have so named it because it works with and is administered to the whole person. This colour is ascertained through dowsing or through kinesiology and is applied, using the reflexology colour instrument, through both feet or by placing the left hand on the sole of the patient's right foot and the right hand on the sole of the left foot and channelling the colour.

Integrating the
Two Therapies

Prior to a first treatment, a patient's medical history is recorded. This includes details of current and past medication, surgical procedures undergone and previous illnesses. The person's current state of health and reason for seeking treatment are noted. To aid me in helping a patient find and work with the cause of the manifested disease, he or she is then given the opportunity to talk about personal issues. The treatment procedure is explained and the patient informed that during it he or she may choose to relax, sleep or talk.

Then a full reflexology treatment is given. This is diagnostic and reveals the painful reflexes. Colour is subsequently applied to these reflexes through the Colour Reflexology Torch. (see below). This torch has a round quartz crystal head and comes with nine stained-glass discs: the head will accommodate two discs at any one time, giving a wide range of colours.

THE COLOUR REFLEXOLOGY TORCH.

When the appropriate coloured disc is inserted and the torch turned on, the round crystal is filled with colour. With this the tender reflex is massaged gently for approximately one minute with the treatment colour and one minute with the complementary colour. To sensitive reflexes associated with a physically manifested disease, the appropriate treatment colour followed by its complementary is administered. To sensitive reflexes not associated with a physical disease, the general colour followed by its complementary is applied.

The chakra points on the spinal reflex of the right foot are then dowsed, first for imbalances then to ascertain whether the imbalance is due to the chakra being over- or under-active. Over-active chakras are treated, on the spinal reflex of both feet, with the chakra's complementary colour. For example, if the base chakra were over-active it would be treated with green, the complementary colour to red. An under-active chakra would be treated, on both feet, with its vibratory colour – thus an under-active throat chakra would be treated with blue, the colour it normally vibrates to (see chart on page 43).

To complete the treatment the patient's overall colour is dowsed. For this a copy of the twelve-colour wheel (see page 44) and a pendulum (see page 48) are needed. Holding the patient's foot, place your pendulum over the colour wheel and ask for the overall colour. The pendulum will swing diagonally across two colours – for example, orange and blue. You then ask the pendulum if orange is the overall colour. If it indicates yes, orange is the overall colour and blue the complementary. If it indicates no, blue is the overall colour and orange the complementary. The overall colour, with its complementary, is then administered to both feet.

Administering colour

Colour can be administered in two ways. You can place the palm of your left hand on the sole of the patient's right foot and the palm of your right hand on their left sole and visualize first the overall colour, then the complementary colour, being channelled through your hands into the feet. Normally, 5 minutes is spent visualizing each colour. Alternatively, the Reflexology Colour Instrument can be used (see opposite). This instrument comprises two boxes and a time controller. Each box contains two compartments. The filters for the overall colour are placed in the two top compartments and the filters for the complementary colour are housed in the lower compartments. One box is then positioned in front of the left foot and one in front of the right foot. The colour and its complementary are administered automatically through a special time sequence that lasts for just under 7 minutes. This instrument should, preferably, be used in a darkened room, as a well-lit room will dilute the colour.

After treatment, patients are advised to work with their overall colour for the next six days. They may be given a visualization or a colour breathing exercise to use. Ideas for these are given throughout the book. They might also be asked to wear appropriately coloured clothes or to lie under a full-length piece of cotton or silk material, in a light room, for 20 minutes. In this case white must be worn under the filter colour. Light filtering through, say, a blue dress and then through yellow underwear would produce not blue but a blend of the two colours – green. Refer also to the section on Self-help With Colour at the end of the book.

Patients might also be given tablets solarised with the necessary overall and complementary colours, kept separately in two black pots to stop the light diluting them. They should be taken for six consecutive days, the overall colour half an hour before breakfast and the complementary colour half an hour before lunch. I have found solarised tablets an effective way of getting patients to work with the required colours, because they are doing what they have been conditioned to do – take a tablet twice a day! When given visualization or any other exercise, patients usually practise for a couple of days and then lapse, due to lack of time or forgetfulness.

THE REFLEXOLOGY INSTRUMENT.

LIGHT BOX AND SET OF NINE STAINED-GLASS PIECES.

Dowsing

It is speculated that the art of dowsing originated from Shamanism. When the Shaman wished to acquire advice from the spirits concerning present difficulties, he would use a stone hung on a string, or a stick rather like a magician's wand, to direct questions at. The direction in which the pebble or stick moved answered 'yes' or 'no' to his question.

A descendant of the Shaman's stick is the forked hazel twig, a device used today to dowse for water, oil and missing objects.

In the 1920s a French priest, Abbé Mermet, author of *Principles and Practice of Radiesthesia*, claimed to have used the art of dowsing to locate and diagnose illness. The Abbé was a member of a religious group and this allowed him access to hospitals to demonstrate his skill. The accuracy of his diagnosis of patients selected by the hospitals' doctors, often surprised onlookers and confounded sceptics.

Dowsing works on the principle that all substances, including the physical body, emit radiation. 'Tuning in' to this radiation enables the body to act as a receiver, causing an intangible energy current to flow through the hands. So, when dowsing for water, oil, or other substances, the pendulum or divining rod is able to locate them by the radiation they emit.

Choosing and preparing a pendulum

Learning to work with a pendulum takes practice and to succeed we must tap into our intuition, trusting any information received. It is important to have your own pendulum. This can be made from crystal, metal or wood. You can use your own ring or pendant suspended on a chain or piece of string. If you buy or are given a pendulum, it should be cleansed of old vibrational energies before you use it. One way of doing this is to leave it in salt water overnight and wash it in running water the following morning. When it has been cleansed, carry it on your person for a couple of weeks to charge it with your own energy.

Finding your 'yes' and 'no'

The first step when working with a pendulum is to discover your own 'yes' and 'no' response. To do this, hold the pendulum in your right or left hand, approximately 15 centimetres/5 inches from your solar plexus and mentally ask it to indicate your 'yes'. It will respond by swinging either clockwise or anti-clockwise or in a diagonal or horizontal line. Now ask it to indicate your 'no'. It will respond by moving in a different direction. If initially the pendulum fails to move, try working with the opposite hand. Remember: to acquire this skill takes patience, practice and trust. Once you have established your 'yes' and 'no', these should not change, provided that you always dowse with the same hand. If you change hands, the response will be reversed. To demonstrate this, hold your pendulum over the palm of your left hand. It will swing either in a clockwise or anti-clockwise direction. Now hold the pendulum over the palm of your right hand and it will swing in the opposite direction. The same applies to the front and back of your hand.

Using a witness

When dowsing for someone who is not physically present, something which holds their vibration (frequently referred to as a 'witness') is needed. This can be a photograph, a piece of their hair or a sample of their handwriting. If you are dowsing a colour for them, place their witness beneath the colour wheel and follow the instructions given on page 46.

A CRYSTAL PENDULUM.

Exercises

1. For this exercise you will need swatches of small pieces of coloured material. Place these on a table and ask your friends or members of your family to mentally select and visualize the colour they are drawn towards. Placing your hand on a hand of each participant in turn, dowse to discover the colour each one has chosen. If you get only one or two right or, indeed, fail to get any right, don't be disheartened. Remember, practice makes perfect.

2. For this exercise you will need a piece of paper, a pencil, eight cups marked 1 to 8 and small pieces of material in eight different colours.
Place one piece of material beneath each of the eight cups and then shuffle the cups around. Now use your pendulum to dowse over each of the cups to discover which colour lies underneath it. As you dowse each colour, write it on the paper with the number of the cup it was under. When you have dowsed all eight cups, check how many you got right. Again, don't be disheartened if you managed to get only one or two. Remember, to become proficient in this art takes time and patience, and leaves no room for self-doubt.

Solarisation

The word 'solar' pertains to the energy from the sun's rays and solarisation involves using those rays to imbue a substance with a required vibrational frequency. In *The Healing Power of Sunlight* Jakob Lorber describes the solarisation of sac lac tablets (pure sea salt) and of the blood of a healthy lamb or calf. Dinsaha P Ghadiali describes in his book how to solarise water with colour, using the device he invented.

Solarised water

To solarise water with a frequency's colour, a box is required which is designed to take stained glass filters at its top and front. The coloured filters are inserted into the box after a glass of spring water has been placed inside. The box is then left in daylight for approximately 1 hour on a bright sunny day or 4 hours on a cloudy, grey day. Small quantities of the water are then taken over several days. There are a couple of

disadvantages with this method. First, the solarised water must be kept in a black, lidded container in the fridge; secondly, the water has a short shelf life. This is a powerful way of working with colour but, for long-term use, is viable only for colour practitioners treating themselves because they are able to solarise fresh water when needed.

An interesting experiment is to charge each of twelve glasses of spring water with one of the twelve colours and then try to taste the difference between them. I found the difference in taste very marked, convincing me that the water had changed.

Solarised tablets

A more practical way of prescribing colour is through solarised tablets. The tablets I use are

SOLARISING BOX.
Sac lac tablets are put in each compartment, under the appropriate stained-glass, and left in the sunlight.

called sac lac and are readily available from large homeopathic pharmacies.

To solarise sac lac tablets, you need a small wooden box with two white compartments, plus a set of stained glass filters that fit over the compartments. Tablets are placed in each compartment and the required stained glass filters are fitted. The box is placed in daylight for the same duration of time used for solarising water. Once solarised, the tablets are placed in black, labelled pots to prevent them losing their colour potency. For a practitioner, it is ideal to have all twelve colours available, each housed in its own pot. The tablets are then available when needed by a patient, and the supply can be replenished on the next sunny day.

The normal dosage is six tablets of the required colour and six of the complementary colour. The required colour is taken half-an-hour before breakfast and the complementary half-an-hour before lunch. One must stress the importance of remembering to take the complementary colour to achieve a balanced treatment. The patient's tablets must be dispensed either in small black pots or in black paper envelopes. Black paper can be obtained from a good art shop. Each envelope must be marked clearly with the colour of the enclosed tablets, the patient's full name, the date and dosage. This is a powerful method of treatment and should be used only by those qualified to integrate colour with reflexology.

It should perhaps be mentioned here that qualified reflexologists choosing to work with integrating these two therapies need to add colour therapy to their insurance. To be able to do this they need to take a recognized, certificated course on how to use colour in conjunction with a reflexology treatment. I must emphasize that practical experience is essential, therefore any course taken must include attendance modules.

Solarised cream

Solarised cream works on the same principle as solarised water. The cream must be pure, free from perfume, chemicals or preservatives. The ideal cream would be home made, though unfortunately this must be kept in a refrigerator, has a short life span and does not take kindly to being left in the sun under stained glass! When a suitable cream has been selected, the desired amount is placed into a white container and a stained glass filter of the required colour is placed over the top. This is then left in the sunlight for several hours. Solarised cream is used primarily for skin conditions.

Solarising crystals

To solarise quartz crystals, put a square of stained-glass of the required colour into the light box (see page 47). Place the crystal on top of the box and switch it on. Leave the crystal to solarise for approximately 10 minutes. Solarised crystals can be held by the patient or can be used to administer colour to the reflex. Crystals must be cleansed after use by leaving them in salt water for several hours.

Working as a Channel for Healing

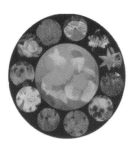

A MANDALA OF FLOWERS.

Each of us has the potential to be a channel for healing. If we choose to realize that potential it can cause dramatic changes in our lives, as old patterns break down so that new ones may be formed – often a very uncomfortable process. Dedicating ourselves as channels involves learning to flow with the energies of life, not knowing where they are leading us. Through this experience we have to learn to trust in the Divine Being – God, Buddha, Universal Intelligence, whatever name each of us calls this supreme power – believing that we will be looked after and given what we need when it is needed.

Healing ourselves

Having decided to become a channel for healing, we must first learn to heal ourselves. I personally believe that any form of therapy we choose to practise requires initial self-healing before we are able to go out and help others. Healing ourselves involves discipline. It requires us to look at our diet, lifestyle, and the state of our emotional and mental bodies.

The majority of us abuse our physical body, taking it so much for granted that we are no longer aware of it. We notice it only if there is pain and disorder. Then, to relieve our symptoms, we go to the doctor and resort to drugs, which can have side effects, creating further disharmony. Very few of us take time to stop and listen to our body. Illness is the body's

way of telling us that we are doing something wrong. I believe that sickness, looked at in this way, can create a great opportunity for spiritual growth. Having said this, I must reiterate that conventional medicine does have its place and can work extremely well alongside complementary therapies.

The therapeutic touch

In *Therapeutic Touch*, Dolores Krieger explains that to channel energy and work with therapeutic touch we must first centre our own consciousness – an act of self-searching, of going within to explore our deeper levels. She believes that this act of inward journeying teaches us to trace or follow the energy flow of our own consciousness in a quest to understand our unique being and our relationship with the universe.

When channelling the vibrational energies of colour, we visualize red, orange and yellow coming into our body through our feet, down through the arms and into our hands and fingers. Green enters diagonally into the heart chakra and blue, indigo and violet enter through the top of the head.

In order to channel these colours, I believe that initially we need to become sensitive to their vibrational frequencies. Because we are beings of light, becoming sensitive to the frequencies that constitute light is another way of exploring our deeper levels.

Exercise for colour sensitivity

This exercise is one way in which sensitivity may be developed. You will need twelve small pieces of material, one for each of the colours of the twelve-colour wheel (see below). Alternatively, you may choose to use flowers and/or crystals in each of these twelve colours. Find yourself a quiet, warm place and sit either on the floor or on a chair, placing your materials on the floor beside you. Working with each colour separately, place the piece of material or flower or crystal into the palm of your left hand. Hold the palm of your right hand approximately 19 centimetres/6 inches above the chosen object. Closing your eyes, try to feel, through the minor chakra in the palm of your right hand, the vibrational energy of the colour you are working with. Make a note of what you experience. Repeat with the remaining colours. If you choose to work with a partner, close your eyes and allow your partner to place one of the coloured objects into your hand, then guess which colour you are holding. If initially you don't feel anything, don't be disheartened. As in all things, learning to feel colour takes time and practice.

After experiencing each colour, place your hands on the ground and ask that the vibrational energy of that colour be laid to the earth. If this is not done, the colours' vibrations will mingle and you will not be able to discern one from the other.

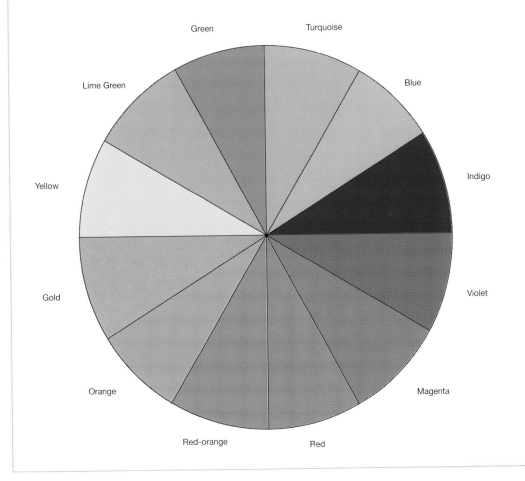

Guidelines for Meditation

Meditation is a discipline that teaches us to relax the body and quieten the mind in order to contact our divine or true self.

The beginner can encounter many difficulties. The first is disciplining him- or herself to set aside time each day to practise. The second is learning to sit still and relax the body. The third is quieting the mind, which most people find extremely difficult. Under normal circumstances, our mind rules us – a situation which, in meditation, we are trying to reverse.

You can achieve this reversal in several ways: through mantras (the repetition of a special sound); yantras (geometric forms); concentration on the breath; listening to music; using imagery. I would recommend that you try a variety of techniques, then select the one you find most beneficial. The ideal way to start is to join a meditation group. This offers support, encouragement and protection during the initial stages of learning.

It is important to develop the habit of setting aside the same time each day for your meditation. Find a quiet, warm place where you will not be disturbed. If necessary, take the telephone off the hook. This is a special time, which you have created for yourself and your own inner development. Light a candle and dedicate it to whichever deity or path you have chosen to follow. If you sit on a chair, have both feet on the floor, hands resting on your knees, palms facing down. Your spine must be straight, your head and neck relaxed and your eyes closed. If you are sitting on the floor, you can sit in full or half lotus, in simple crossed-leg posture, or against the wall with your legs out straight. Again, it is important that your spine is upright: it represents a golden shaft of light which earths you to this planet but which can also lift you up into the higher realms of consciousness.

Let go of any thoughts that come into your mind. Visualize them as beautiful bubbles which float up into the atmosphere and gently disperse. Once your mind is quiet and still, bring your concentration into your physical body. Move slowly through it starting with your feet and working up to your head, releasing any tension in the muscles and organs. If your body feels uncomfortable, change its position. Then bring your concentration into your breath. Slowly breathe in to five and out to five, allowing your mind to become still. With body and mind relaxed, begin your chosen meditation or visualization.

In meditation we are working with the seven main chakras. These are gateways leading us into higher states of consciousness. They open when we are in a meditative state, and it is important that we close them at the end of each meditation. If this is not done, we are leaving open doors through which unwelcome energies can enter. To close them, visualize each chakra as an open lotus flower. Starting with the crown chakra, mentally work down all seven chakras, visualizing each flower closing back to a bud. On completing this, gradually increase your rate of breathing, becoming aware of your physical body and where it is placed. When you feel ready, slowly open your eyes, stretch your hands over your head, then continue with the activities of the day.

The meditations and visualizations given throughout this book are aimed at practitioners and those interested in working with colour, but practitioners might like to use them with their patients to help them to work with the colour they require.

Crystal meditation

This is a meditation for spiritual energy and can be used at the beginning of a therapy session.

Imagine that you are sitting in a glass chalice. This chalice is bulb shaped, wide at the bottom and narrow at the top, similar to a brandy glass. It is made in such a way that it reflects all the spectral colours. These colours dance in the space between your body and the chalice, interacting with your aura. The chalice is strong and forms a protective web around you.

Looking up to the opening at the chalice's top, visualize a shaft of white, divine light flooding into your body, through your crown chakra, penetrating any part of you where there is dis-ease or pain. It pours down until you are completely filled with light, energy, peace and joy, enabling you to become a strong channel for healing. Spend a few moments basking in this energizing, healing light. Then thank the spiritual world for the gift you have just received.

SEATED MEDITATION POSTURE.

CROSS-LEGGED
MEDITATION POSTURE.

Violet

Violet is the colour related to spirituality. In Christianity it is the colour given to God the Father and is used in ceremonies and rituals throughout Lent and Advent. It is a colour associated with priestly rule and authority and is the colour of truth, fasting and penitence. It is said by some to be the colour assigned to St Mary Magdalene. The Romans connected violet with Jupiter, the god of thunder, rain and storm.

When we relate this colour to ourselves, it stands for self-respect and dignity, a colour frequently needed by those who have no respect for their own thoughts, feelings or physical body. Violet is also related to insight and the higher self.

Violet is the dominant colour of the crown chakra. The endocrine gland associated with this chakra is the pineal gland. In the aura, a deep purple denotes high spiritual attainment and holy love. It proclaims the divine radiance. A pale lilac shows cosmic consciousness and love for humanity and a bluish purple signifies transcendent idealism.

Violet can be a very beneficial colour for psychological disorders such as schizophrenia and manic depression. It also helps diseases of the scalp and is good for combating viral and bacterial infections. On an emotional level, those suffering a 'broken heart' can be helped when this colour is applied to the heart chakra alongside rose pink. Violet, the shade taken from the amethyst crystal, mends the broken heart and rose pink fills it with unconditional love.

The pineal gland

The pineal gland is a small, reddish-grey structure about the size of a pea. It is situated between the under surface of the cerebrum and the mid-brain, just in front of the cerebellum.

Its main secretion is melatonin, which works with the body's biological clock. Other substances found in the pineal gland include norepinephrine, serotonin, gamma aminobutyric acid and gonadotropin-releasing hormones.

The reflex is situated on both feet and on both hands. On the feet it is located on the inner side of the big toe, approximately 1.2 centimetres/½ inch from the top of the toe and on the hands it is found on the inner side of the thumb, near the top.

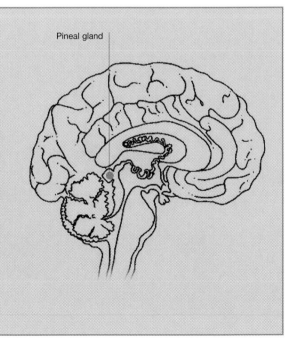

Pineal gland

REFLEXES ASSOCIATED WITH THE COLOUR VIOLET

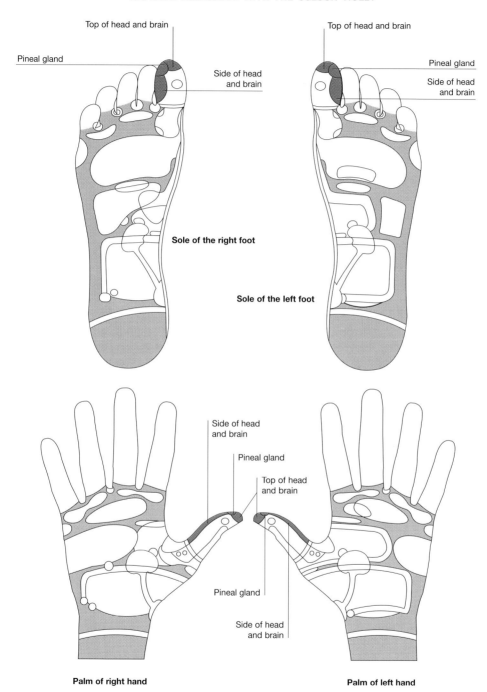

Top of head and brain

Pineal gland

Side of head
and brain

Top of head and brain

Pineal gland

Side of head
and brain

Sole of the right foot

Sole of the left foot

Side of head
and brain

Pineal gland

Top of head
and brain

Pineal gland

Side of head
and brain

Palm of right hand

Palm of left hand

REFLEXES ASSOCIATED WITH THE COLOUR VIOLET

Back of left hand

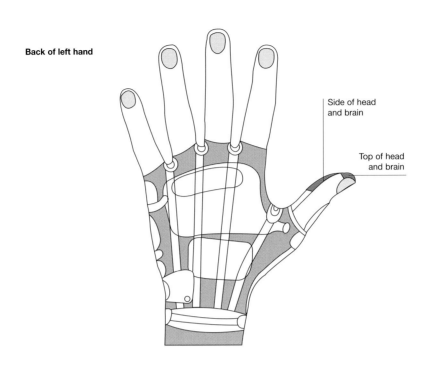

Side of head and brain

Top of head and brain

Back of right hand

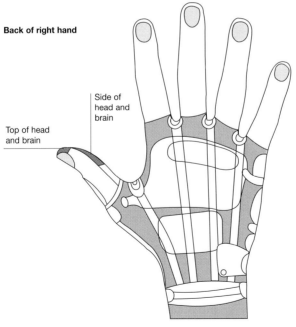

Side of head and brain

Top of head and brain

Reflexes associated with the colour violet

Medial side of right foot

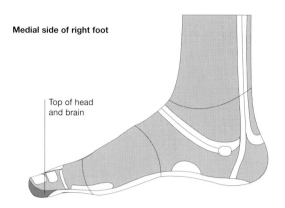

Top of head
and brain

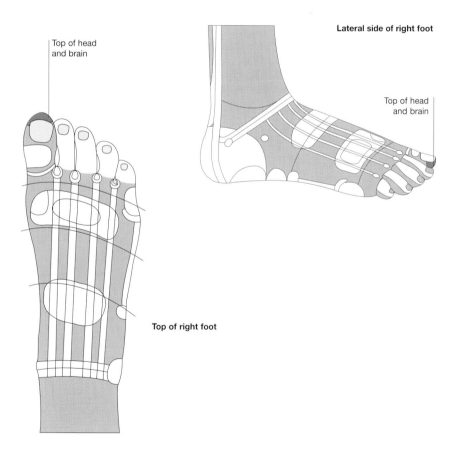

Top of head
and brain

Lateral side of right foot

Top of head
and brain

Top of right foot

REFLEXES ASSOCIATED WITH THE COLOUR VIOLET

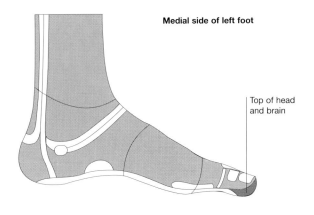

Medial side of left foot

Top of head
and brain

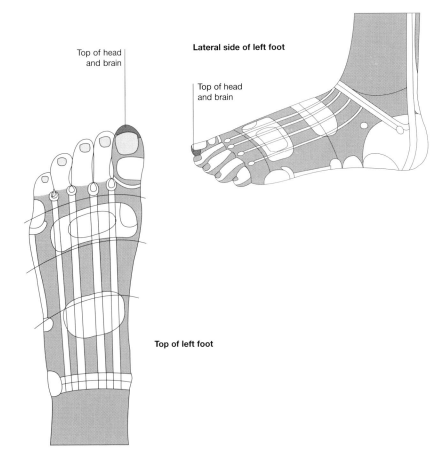

Lateral side of left foot

Top of head
and brain

Top of head
and brain

Top of head
and brain

Top of left foot

Associated Reflexes

Brain

Protected by its thick bony case, the skull, the brain is divided into three main parts, the cerebral hemispheres, the cerebellum and the brain stem. The cerebral hemispheres control speech, memory and intelligence and the cerebellum controls the co-ordination of movement and balance. The brain stem merges into the top of the spinal cord and maintains our breathing and circulation. Nerve signals travel up and down the spinal cord, which links the brain to the rest of the body.

The reflex to the brain is located on the top and half way down the distal aspect of both large toes and thumbs.

Scalp

This is the soft covering on top of the skull. It consists of five layers. The first is the skin, covered with its own layer of hair; the second is fat; the third a layer of fibrous tissue; the fourth a loose layer of connective tissue; the fifth, another fibrous layer, clinging closely to the skull.

The reflex for the scalp is located across the top of both big toes and both thumbs.

Circulatory system

The circulatory system comprises the heart, arteries and veins and its work is to carry blood to and from every part of our body. The arteries carry oxygenated blood away from the heart: veins return blood to the heart. The blood makes two separate circuits from and to the heart. In the shorter of these circuits (pulmonary circulation) 'used' blood is pumped to the lungs where it takes in oxygen and expels carbon dioxide. It then returns to the heart. From the heart, the oxygenated blood is pumped throughout the body (systemic circulation) in order to supply all tissues with nutrients and to pick up waste products before returning to the heart to be re-oxygenated in the pulmonary circulation.

The blood is the body's transport system. It is composed of red corpuscles, produced by the bone marrow; white corpuscles, produced by the bone marrow and lymphoid tissue; and platelets, which play an important role in blood coagulation. The white corpuscles are involved in combating infection, wound healing and rejection of foreign bodies and platelets.

I personally believe that the energy our blood vibrates to is akin to the violet ray. My theory is based on quantum physics and on the work of Samoilova (see page 34).

A note on treatment colours

Treatment colours given for specific ailments have been formulated in various ways: some from the experience of other practitioners, such as Ronald Hunt; some through my own experience with patients over many years; some from the insight of quantum physics, while a small percentage of colours have been found with dowsing. The treatment colours given for specific diseases throughout the chapters work with approximately 90 per cent of the population, but the other 10 per cent will need a different colour (this is similar to conventional medicine). If you can work with your intuition you will know the correct colour to use. If in doubt, dowse using the twelve-colour wheel.

Treatment Colours
for Common Ailments

Pineal gland

Seasonal Affective Disorder (SAD)
This is caused by an excess of melatonin in the blood during the daylight hours. Symptoms include depression, lethargy and a craving for carbohydrates. (Also see page 33.)
To treat: To help this condition, use yellow and its complementary violet on the pineal reflex. Also suggest that the sufferer invests in a SAD lamp.

Brain

Amnesia (loss of memory) Amnesia can result from deep emotional shock or trauma, or occur for no apparent reason. More generally it stems from a blow to the head, which can damage the brain if severe enough.
To treat: To help this condition, use violet with its complementary yellow on the brain reflex.

Headaches and migraine
Physiologically there are two causes for head pain. The first is tension deriving from strain on facial, neck and scalp muscles; the second is the swelling of local blood vessels resulting in strain within their walls. Other factors are stress, too little or too much sleep, overeating or drinking, a noisy, stuffy environment. It can also be the symptom of an underlying disorder.

Migraine is a severe headache, which can be preceded by other symptoms such as blurred vision. Some neurologists believe that the arteries to the brain become first narrowed then swollen, possibly a reaction to a trigger factor such as cheese or chocolate.
To treat: For ordinary headaches and migraine treat the head reflex with indigo and its complementary gold.

Epilepsy This condition results from a problem in the brain's communication system. Information is transferred within the brain as electrical impulses which pass from cell to cell. As each brain cell 'fires', it stimulates its neighbouring cell: this, in turn, fires and stimulates further cells.

If the brain cells are more excitable than usual, they will fire more easily creating a sudden burst of abnormal electrical activity within cell groups. This produces what is termed a seizure, which may be partial – limited to just part of the brain, or general – affecting a larger portion of the brain.
To treat: A normal reflexology treatment is not recommended because it can trigger an attack. Treat the head reflexes on both feet with colour alone, using indigo and gold and applying the general colours only to the remaining reflexes.

Scalp

Dandruff The two main causes of the scalp's excessive production of small flakes of dead skin are a mild form of eczema and psoriasis of the scalp.
To treat: Treat the scalp reflex with yellow and its complementary violet.

Circulatory system

High blood pressure 'Essential' hypertension can be hereditary and is also influenced by our lifestyle. 'Secondary' hypertension can result from other conditions such as kidney disease and hormonal disorders.

To treat: The treatment colours to be applied through both feet are blue followed by its complementary orange.

Low blood pressure (Hypotension) Postural hypotension is the most common type, caused when rising too quickly from a sitting or lying position. The result is dizziness. Occasionally, postural hypotension can occur with certain diseases – diabetes mellitus, for example.

To treat: The treatment colours to be applied through both feet are red followed by its complementary green .

Anaemia This occurs when the amount of haemoglobin in the blood falls. The symptoms include pallor, weakness, fainting, breathlessness and palpitations. The causes can be many, including a severe deficiency of vitamin B12 or folic acid. All cases of anaemia should be medically investigated to ascertain the cause.

To treat: The treatment colours to be applied through both feet are violet followed by its complementary yellow.

MRSA Methicillin Resistant Staphylococcus Aureus and VRE (Vancomycin resistant enterococci) are the most commonly encountered multidrug-resistant organisms.

Hospital patients are more vulnerable to MRSA infection because they are unwell or may have surgical wounds. When treating someone suffering from this disease, good, basic hygiene precautions must be adhered to.

To treat: The treatment colours to apply through both feet are violet followed by its complementary yellow. In addition, tablets solarised with the two colours should be given for fourteen days.

Reflex	Condition	Treatment Colour	Complementary Colour
Pineal gland	SAD		
Brain	Amnesia		
	Headaches & migraine		
	Epilepsy		
Scalp	Dandruff		
Circulatory system	High blood pressure		
	Low blood pressure		
	Anaemia		
	MRSA		

The Crown Chakra

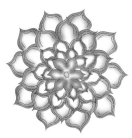

This centre's Sanskrit name is 'Sahasrara' which means 'thousandfold'. It is located at the crown of the head, is regarded as the centre of infinity, and is generally symbolized by a thousand-petalled white or violet lotus flower. The lotus's petals are arranged in twenty rows and each row of fifty petals contains, written in white, the fifty letters of the Sanskrit alphabet. It is believed that the fifty sounds produced from these letters interact with specific parts of the physical body and with our emotional and psychological states of being. Some esoteric schools furnish this chakra with just 960 petals, making the central petals golden and the 948 surrounding them violet or white.

At a physical level, this chakra is connected with the pineal gland, nervous system and brain. The physical symptoms that can arise when this chakra is not in balance are brain disease, migraines, disorders of the endocrine system and psychological problems. Too much energy here can cause a constant sense of frustration, while too little energy makes us indecisive with no spark of joy in life.

Each major chakra (excluding the alta major), is full of symbolism and is connected with gods and goddesses, animals, geometric forms, colours and mantras, making a rich tapestry for further study. In their various created forms, the chakras have been recognized as a vital part of our being for many generations, but it was Hinduism that clothed them with their

many images. One particularly interesting symbol is the one used by the medical profession – the caduceus. This symbol portrays the seven chakras intertwined by a black and a white snake representing the two main *nadis*, the *ida* and *pingala*. Does this mean, I wonder, that early medical practitioners also recognized these energy centres and their important role in our overall well-being?

The crown chakra represents the top rung of our spiritual ladder and is the place where our lower and higher selves are united, leading us to experience the indescribable bliss of union with the divine reality. It is the centre of pure consciousness and the abode of the god Shiva. Shiva is the aspect of Divine power responsible for raising man from physical bondage to spiritual enlightenment. When the *kundalini* energy, Shakti – the goddess principle of power that lies dormant in the base chakra – rises through the *sushumna*, she and Shiva are united, bringing about a transformation in human consciousness. This union symbolizes the integration of our duality into wholeness. Through this union we attain the realization of who we truly are. One of the questions yoga students ask themselves is 'Who am I?' The answer takes many lifetimes to discover because the 'I' that we are seeking has nothing to do with the physical body but is that divine spark within each of us that has no beginning and no ending.

When the crown chakra is opened and illumination takes place, the brow and crown chakras unite to form the halo depicted in the pictures of saints and enlightened beings. At this stage we view our spirituality in a very personal way that is not tied up with any dogma. Unlike the lower five chakras, this and the brow chakra contain no mantra or element.

When this chakra is open and functioning to its full potential, we become open to divine energy. This enables us to transcend the laws of nature and have total access to the subconscious and unconscious mind. The way to work with this chakra is through meditation. (See the section on Guidelines for Meditation, pages 54–55.)

The crown chakra reflex on the feet and hands

The reflex for the crown chakra is found on the top of each big toe and each thumb. To check this chakra for imbalances, place your finger either on the top of the big toe or on top of the thumb where the reflex for the chakra is situated. Now, with your pendulum in your other hand, dowse to discover if this chakra is in balance, or if it is under- or over-active. If it is under-active treat with violet; if over-active treat with yellow.

To treat, use either the reflexology torch or place your finger on the reflex point and channel the required colour through yourself.

THE POSITION OF THE CROWN CHAKRA REFLEX ON THE FEET AND HANDS

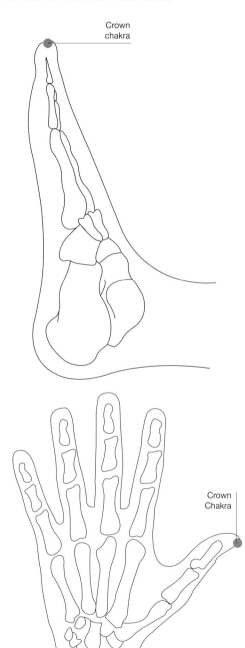

Crown chakra

Crown Chakra

Visualization with Violet

It is a sunny, warm autumn day and you are standing outside a small temple, situated in the heart of the countryside. Fields divided by hedges and containing an assortment of trees surround the temple. The trees are wearing their autumnal colours and those leaves that have fallen create a rich, multi-coloured mosaic carpet upon the earth. Birds sing overhead and there is the occasional lowing of cattle as they graze in nearby fields.

Walking up to the door of the temple, push it open and walk through. Inside the air is faintly scented and feels cool in comparison with the warmth of the sun outside. You become aware of the stillness and silence of this place and you allow this atmosphere of peace and calm to enter every aspect of your being.

As your eyes become accustomed to the comparative darkness, your attention turns to the beautiful stained glass windows. As the sun shines through these, shafts of coloured light play upon the walls and floor.

Around the centre of the temple are chairs. Go and sit on one that is flooded with violet light. Bathing your body in this colour and absorbing it through your eyes gives you the dignity and self-respect that each one of us should have as human beings. These feelings raise you to a higher level of consciousness where you are allowed to glimpse your true self, the eternal part of you that has no beginning and no ending. You are given the understanding that this is the real you and that your physical body is the sacred instrument in which you live on the earth plane. You realize what a very beautiful instrument the physical body is, capable of self-healing when given the right conditions. You are told to respect the sacredness of life and, as a channel for healing, to be open to the healing power of the universe.

Before leaving the temple, sit for a while feeling and absorbing this colour and reflecting upon these thoughts.

Meditation with the Crown Chakra

When working with visualization or meditation, remember to follow the basic practice given in Guidelines for Meditation on pages 54–55.

This meditation utilizes the dodecahedron: it is one of five platonic solids, and is affiliated with the ether or *akasha*. The term 'Platonic' is a reference to the philosopher Plato who, in his work *Timaeus*, uses this term to describe a universal cosmology based upon interlocking patterns of geometry.

Pythagoras, who named them the perfect solids, used these patterns two hundred years earlier. They are the only volumes that have all outer angles and interior angles equal. The other four are: the hexahedron, related to the earth element; the tetrahedron, related to the fire element; the octahedron, related to the air element; and the icosahedron, related to the water element.

Sitting quietly, imagine yourself inside a violet dodecahedron. Take note of the twenty points that form part of its construction and feel the effect its shape and colour has upon

you. Bringing your concentration to your crown chakra, visualize this as an open lotus flower that is being filled with a rich golden light coming from the universe. Imagine this light flowing from your crown chakra and down the centre of your spine, and then engulfing you in an orb of golden light.

As this light radiates out from your spine, each of the twenty points on the dodecahedron ignite, their light encompassing the room in which you sit, your home, your friends and family, the animal, plant and bird kingdom. As you watch this spectacle, you feel your own vibrational frequency become heightened to a new level of awareness, and you are made to understand that the frequency of all those you have surrounded with this light has also been raised. You begin to see things in a different perspective and feel as if you have just awakened from a dream into reality.

This is a good meditation with which to start each day.

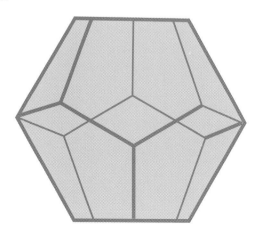

Indigo

This colour was originally derived from the leaves of the indigo plant, which is found worldwide. Unlike other natural dyes indigo has a natural fastness to light and water and needs no mordent to fix it.

Indigo is the colour of dusk, the colour given to 'the vaults of heaven' at the time when daylight fades to make way for the darkness of night. This is thought by many to be a romantic time, known in France as *l'heure bleu* when ladies entertained their lovers and husbands called on their mistresses.

This colour comprises blue and violet and is the dominant colour of the brow chakra. The endocrine gland associated with this chakra is the pituitary, known as the master gland of the body. Indigo also encompasses our organs of sight and hearing and embraces other aspects of our face such as our sinuses and teeth.

Combining both the blue and violet ray, indigo speaks of deep devotion allied to a sense of dignity and unconditional love. The properties of the indigo ray can help us to foster transcendent vision and an ability to hear the voice of our own intuition. Spiritually, the brow chakra has a close connection with the alta major chakra and our physical eyes. The alta major chakra (known as the 'mouth of God') is where life force (the breath of God) enters the body; the brow centre is where, through the practice of meditation, we perceive the light of God, the door to higher consciousness. When we are able to unite the brow and the alta major

The pituitary gland

The pituitary gland is a peanut-sized organ lying in a bony hollow in the base of the skull and is the most important endocrine gland in the body. (Endocrine glands are composed of hormone-producing cells clustered around blood vessels.) The pituitary comprises an anterior and posterior lobe and produces many of the hormones necessary for the body's growth, development and everyday maintenance. The release of hormones from the anterior lobe is controlled by the hypothalamus: this is the part of the brain situated just above the pituitary and often referred to as the body's light meter. This reflex is found in the centre of the fleshy pad on the toes and thumbs.

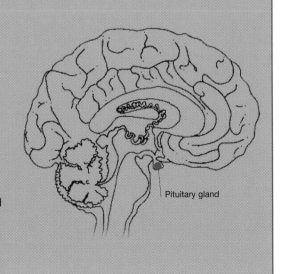

Pituitary gland

centres, they create, together with the physical eyes, a triangle of light that then shines out through our eyes, the mirrors of our soul.

Indigo has the power to create an impression of infinite space and timelessness and can create for us the conditions needed for self-reflection and contemplation. In some people, however, this could induce a sense of solitude or isolation, and therefore it is advisable to work carefully with this colour. In some cases indigo can trigger depression, or intensify it in a person already suffering from this complaint.

Found at the cool end of the spectrum, the indigo ray is cooling and astringent. It has the capacity to induce anaesthesia in the physical body, making it a powerful painkiller. It is a colour that helps to purify both the blood stream and the psychic currents found in the aura. It can relieve muscular strains or tension, help neuralgic pain and relieve insomnia. It is also a colour that is helpful in treating nosebleeds.

Because of its connection to our organs of sight and hearing, indigo is a colour used to treat cataracts and deafness. If we suffer from either of these complaints we should look for the cause of the physical disease.

A problem relating to the eye can be a structural defect or the result of an accident. Another possibility, however, could be our unwillingness to see things that are beneficial for us, or a refusal to see someone else's point of view. This attitude could lead to a persecution complex, making our outlook on life warped.

In the same way, deafness can be caused by an accident, severe shock, or being constantly subjected to high pitched sounds such as those of high-speed drills used by dental surgeons. But deafness could also stem from our unwillingness to hear suggestions made for our own good. In such a case, we are giving our subconscious a silent command to shut our ears.

REFLEXES ASSOCIATED WITH THE COLOUR INDIGO

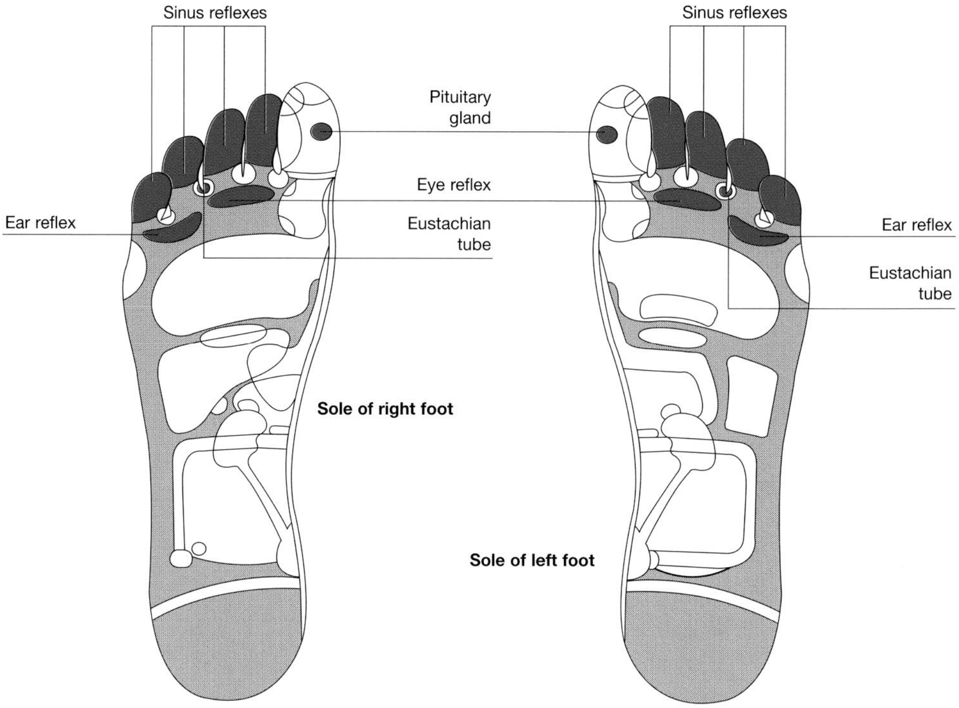

Sinus reflexes

Sinus reflexes

Pituitary gland

Eye reflex

Ear reflex

Eustachian tube

Ear reflex

Eustachian tube

Sole of right foot

Sole of left foot

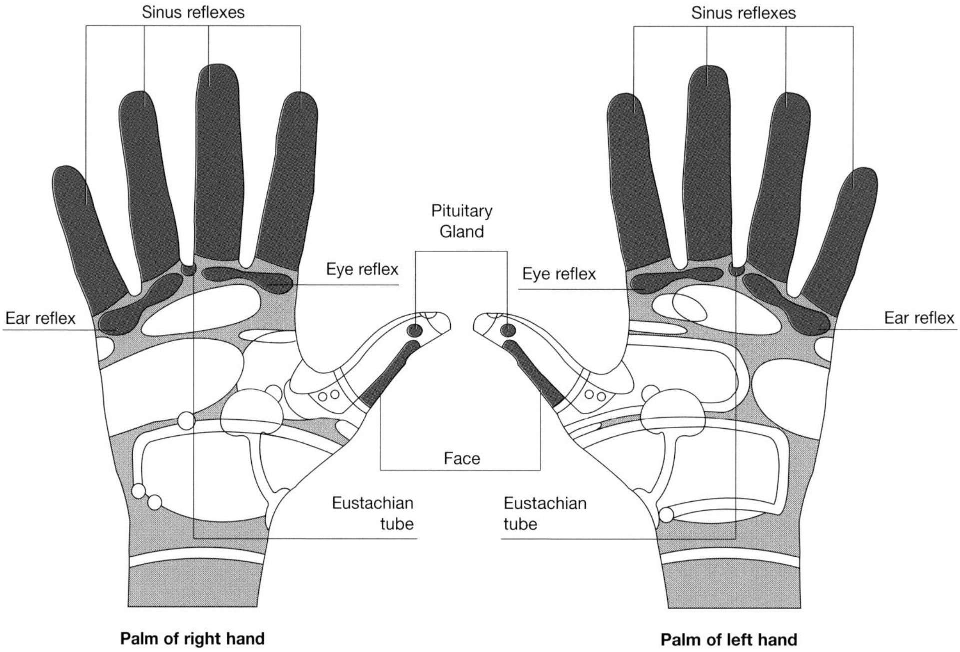

Sinus reflexes

Sinus reflexes

Pituitary Gland

Eye reflex

Eye reflex

Ear reflex

Ear reflex

Face

Eustachian tube

Eustachian tube

Palm of right hand

Palm of left hand

REFLEXES ASSOCIATED WITH THE COLOUR INDIGO

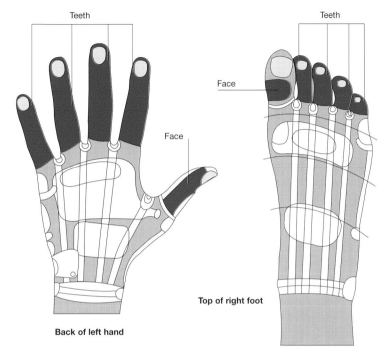

Teeth

Teeth

Face

Back of left hand

Top of right foot

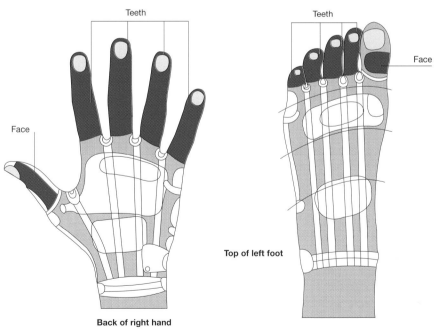

Teeth

Teeth

Face

Face

Back of right hand

Top of left foot

Associated Reflexes

Face

The reflex for this is found on the fronts of the big toes and the thumbs and covers all parts of the face, including the mouth and nose.

Sinuses

Sinuses are air-filled cavities in the bones of the face and skull and are linked by narrow channels to the nose. They are responsible for reducing the weight of the head and giving resonance to the voice.

The reflexes are found on the pads of all four small toes and fingers.

Ears

Our ears give us our sense of hearing and of equilibration and equilibrium. The outer ear contains the cells that produce lubricating wax. It collects sound waves, funnelling them along the outer ear canal. The middle ear receives these sound waves and passes them to the inner ear. The middle ear contains the eustachian tube, which channels air from the nose to the middle ear chamber, to keep the pressure on the inside of the ear drum equal to that on the outside. The inner ear converts sound waves to nerve impulses and transmits them to the brain. It is also responsible for controlling our balance.

The reflexes are found in zones 2 and 3 at the base of the second and third toes and fingers.

Teeth

The function of our teeth is to bite and grind food and to aid our clarity of speech. Each tooth comprises enamel, dentine, cementum, pulp and periodontal membrane.

The reflexes for the teeth are found on the fronts of all ten toes and fingers. 1st incisor reflexes are on the front of the big toes and thumbs. 2nd incisors and canine teeth reflexes are on the front of the second toes and fingers. 1st and 2nd premolar reflexes are on the front of the third toes and fingers. 1st and 2nd molar reflexes are on the front of the fourth toes and fingers. 3rd molar (or wisdom teeth) reflexes are on the front of the fifth toes and fingers.

Eyes

The eyes are hollow, spherical organs held within a bony cavity, the orbit. They consist of an outer wall of three main layers and a three-fold central cavity. These three central cavities are filled with a transparent watery fluid responsible for preserving the eyes' shape.

Our eyes are elaborate photoreceptors, detecting information by a series of electro-chemical changes to the brain. The visual cortex is the part of the brain that processes this information.

The inner layer of the eye, the retina, contains light-sensitive cells called rods and cones. The rods are responsible for our black-and-white vision and function best at low light. The cones are responsible for our colour vision and operate at high and medium levels of light.

The reflexes are found in zones 2 and 3 at the base of the fourth and fifth toes and fingers.

Treatment Colours
for Common Ailments

Pituitary gland

Diabetes insipidus This is not to be confused with diabetes mellitus, commonly known as sugar diabetes. This disorder can arise from damage to the pituitary gland resulting from a severe head injury, from surgical procedures, or from pressure on this gland from a pituitary tumour. Anyone suffering from this disorder needs medical treatment alongside complementary therapy.
To treat: Treatment colours are indigo followed by its complementary gold to the pituitary reflex.

Pituitary tumour These almost always occur in the anterior lobe. They can be benign or malignant. They can cause an over-production of the hormone prolactin, and exert pressure on the lobes of the gland and on the nerves to the eyes.
To treat: Work with magenta and its complementary lime green.

Face

Bells palsy This is caused by inflammation and compression of the swollen facial nerve as it passes through a tiny opening in the skull behind the ear in its course to the muscles of the face.
To treat: Use yellow followed by its complementary violet on the face reflex.

Trigeminal neuralgia This is one of the most severe forms of neuralgia, affecting the trigeminal nerve. It is characterized by excruciating pain on one side of the face and can occur many times during a day. The pain is started by touching trigger points around the lips and gums.
To treat: Treatment colours are indigo, followed by its complementary gold, on the face reflex.

Head colds Caused by any one of nearly 200 viruses, these are normally confined to the nose and throat.
To treat: Use orange followed by its complementary blue.

Sinuses

Sinusitis The usual cause of this is an infection of the sinuses often following a cold. The symptoms can include headache and a blocked nose followed by a greenish discharge.
To treat: Use red/orange, followed by its complementary turquoise, on the sinus reflexes of both feet or hands.

Catarrh The most common causes of catarrh are viral infections such as a common cold; others are allergies and nasal polyps. When suffering from this condition, it is advisable to exclude all dairy produce from the diet because this can create mucus in the body.
To treat: When caused by a viral infection use red/orange followed by turquoise. If pain is being experienced, work with indigo and gold.

Ears

Infections of the outer ear These are caused by bacteria and may be localized as a boil or abscess.

To treat: Use red/orange, followed by its complementary turquoise, on the ear reflexes.

Ruptured eardrum This can happen for a variety of reasons: when a sharp object is poked into the ear; from receiving a blow to the ear; as a result of middle ear infection or a fractured skull. A ruptured eardrum normally heals itself within two weeks.
To treat: Use indigo followed by its complementary gold.

Menieres disease This is an increase of fluid in the labyrinth of the inner ear. The pressure can rupture or distort the nerve cells in the labyrinth wall, disturbing our sense of balance. If the cochlea is damaged, our hearing will be adversely affected. In severe cases medical treatment is required.
To treat: Treatment colours are green followed by its complementary red.

Tinnitus Sufferers from this complaint hear, within the ears, noises that do not come from an external source. Damage to the auditory pathway is thought to be the cause, and the most common part of the ear to suffer this damage is the cochlea. Other causes can be a perforated eardrum, general diseases such as high blood pressure, or the effect of taking certain drugs. Sometimes the removal of excess wax from the ears will provide a cure. I have found that treating this complaint with colour gradually diminishes the sound until it is barely audible. However, if the patient suffers stress the ear noise again increases.
To treat: Treatment colours are magenta followed by its complementary lime green.

Teeth
Alveolar abscess This is an infection that arises in or round a tooth and spreads, if not treated, to the surrounding bone.
To treat: Use red/orange and its complementary turquoise.

Gingivitis An inflammation of the gums, which can be acute or chronic. The chronic form usually appears in adulthood and can be progressive. There is pain, and the gums may be ulcerated and bleed easily.
To treat: Use indigo with its complementary gold.

Toothache This is usually caused by decay that has either entered the pulp chamber or is close to doing so. If the decay is not removed, the pulp will die resulting in an apical abscess. For this, and all dental problems, the advice of a dental surgeon should be sought, but colour can be a great help during the interim period and the healing process.
To treat: As an emergency treatment, prior to seeing a dentist, work with indigo and its complementary gold.

Eyes
Conjunctivitis This is an inflammation of the conjunctiva, caused by a bacterial or viral infection, or sometimes by an allergy such as hay fever.
To treat: Work with indigo and its complementary gold.

Glaucoma The cause of this disease is a build-up of aqueous humour in the ciliary body of the eye. It is important that this condition is diagnosed and treated by a medical practitioner in its early stages in order to prevent any loss of vision.

To treat: Work with indigo and its complementary gold.

Stye This is caused by bacteria invading one or more of the follicles that produce the eyelashes.

To treat: Work with red/orange and turquoise. If you are using the reflexology torch, make sure that the light is not shone directly into the patient's eyes.

Eye strain This is due to refractive errors and ocular muscle defects. The symptoms are aching, burning, tearing or a sandy sensation in the eyes. The causes can be long hours spent at a computer, or reading in a bad light.

To treat: Work with green and its complementary red.

Reflex	Condition	Treatment Colour	Complementary Colour
Pituitary gland	Diabetes insipidus		
	Pituitary tumour		
Face	Bells palsy		
	Trigeminal neuralgia		
	Head colds		
Sinuses	Sinusitis		
	Associated pain		
	Catarrh		
	Associated pain		
Ears	Infections of outer ear		
	Ruptured eardrum		
	Menieres disease		
	Tinnitus		
Teeth	Alveolar abscess		
	Gingivitis		
	Toothache		
Eyes	Conjunctivitis		
	Glaucoma		
	Stye		
	Eye strain		

The Brow Chakra

The Sanskrit name for this centre is 'Ajna' which means 'command'. It is situated at the centre of the brow in line with the eyebrows. This centre is responsible for receiving commands from our higher self, via our intuition. The dominant colour of the brow chakra is indigo. Its polarity is creation and destruction. To transcend this polarity is to experience consciousness.

This chakra is composed of ninety-six petals but is depicted with just two. These represent our duality and show our need to integrate this duality into wholeness so that this chakra can fully open. The depiction of two petals is also based on reports by clairvoyants that this chakra appears to them to be divided into two segments.

The brow chakra is our centre for visualization and perception. It reflects the two-fold nature of the mind: the ego self and the spirit self; the reasoning mind and the intuitive mind.

The brow chakra is where the duality of our nature is united to bring about a spiritual awakening, demonstrated by the termination at this centre of the two main *nadis*, the *ida* (masculine) and the *pingala* (feminine). In Indian philosophy this coming together is symbolized by the union of Shakti and Shiva.

Shakti, the feminine principle, is the powerful, latent, *kundalini* energy present in the base chakra. In the brow chakra resides the masculine principle, Shiva. To bring about the state of enlightenment, the Shakti must rise through the *sushumna*, vivifying all the lower chakras on her way to the brow chakra. Here she is united with her masculine counterpart, Shiva, before rising into the enlightenment of the crown chakra.

The brow chakra is sometimes referred to as the third eye because it enables us to see the inner light that is our true self. When meditating, we are encouraged to lift our closed eyes and focus them on this chakra point, because it is here that we first perceive the light. At first it appears as a tiny white speck but, with practice, it grows into an orb of brilliant light. This light is the door through which we must pass to those higher states of consciousness. To perceive this light can take many months or even years of regular meditation practice. If, on the diagram of this chakra, we were to join the upper and lower points of the petals we would form the vesica pisces. In sacred geometry, this shape is related to the light that came out of the original darkness.

When this chakra is balanced and functioning to its full potential we have become detached from material possessions, have overcome the fear of death and are no longer preoccupied with worldly possessions, fame or fortune. Our inherent gifts of astral travel and telepathy become available and we have the ability to access past lives.

If this chakra is over-active it can make us proud, religiously dogmatic, manipulative and an egomaniac. If it is under-active we can become over-sensitive to the feelings of others, non-assertive, afraid of success and unable to distinguish between the ego self and the higher self.

Instability in this chakra can lead to tiredness, sinus problems, headaches, migraine, eye and vision problems, catarrh, hay fever, sleeplessness and mental stress. If a person is suffering from any of these complaints, it is advisable to check for imbalances in this chakra.

The brow chakra reflex on the feet and hands

On the toes and thumbs, the reflex point for the brow chakra is found between the first and second phalanges. To check for imbalances, place your finger on the chakra's reflex on either the foot or hand. Now, with your pendulum in your other hand, dowse to ascertain if this chakra is in balance, or if it is under-active or over-active. If it is under-active, treat with indigo; if over-active, treat with gold.

To treat, either use the reflexology torch or place your finger on the reflex point and channel the required colour.

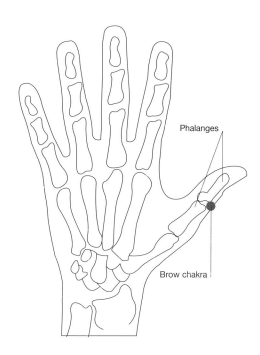

Phalanges

Brow chakra

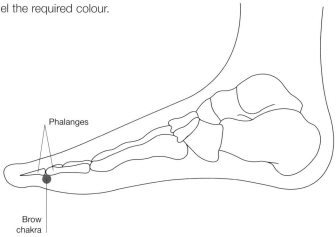

Phalanges

Brow chakra

Visualization with Indigo

The sun's rays are sinking beneath the horizon, anticipating the darkness and silence of night. With the rays of light vanquished, the sky vibrates to the deep indigo of night, wrapping the world in a soft, velvet cloak of peace and silence. Against night's indigo the stars shimmer like diamonds and the moon's halo glows a soft orange and gold.

Imagine yourself to be part of this scene and, as night gently enfolds you all the accumulated tension, strain and stress of the past day is gradually released. The sense of peace and feeling of relaxation that follows creates the inner space needed for the indigo to dissolve any mental or emotional pain you may be suffering. Only when painful issues have been resolved can you walk free.

In the stillness that follows this inner cleansing, visualize a golden shaft of starlight entering your crown chakra. From the crown chakra the light passes through your head to flow gently down your spinal column. You become aware of a pleasant tingling sensation as your nervous system and all the muscles and organs that this system feeds are re-energized. Your body fills with light and you become part of the night's scene, aware now that each star and planet is creating its own sound – that constant, undulating harmony, known as the music of the spheres.

Rest with this visualization for as long as you wish, allowing yourself, if necessary to drift into sleep. If this happens, it is because you need that deep, peaceful sleep which allows the body to rid itself of toxins and repair damaged tissues. When you feel ready to return to everyday awareness, gradually increase your inhalation and exhalation. Visualize each chakra closing, like an open flower returning to a bud, before opening your eyes.

Meditation with the Brow Chakra

The brow chakra is our centre of light, the place where, in a state of deep meditation, we first perceive our own inner divine light. In this meditation, the light from the flame of the candle represents that inner light.

Sit comfortably in a darkened room, with a lighted candle placed at a comfortable viewing distance. Begin by gently breathing in and out to a count of five. This simple exercise releases tension from the body and slows down the constant stream of thoughts bombarding the brain.

When you feel relaxed and your mind has become quiet and still, open your eyes and look at the candle-flame. Its light is a representation of your own inner light. Contemplate your understanding of divine light and consider how you perceive your own

inner light? Do you feel that this light is something separate from you or is it your true self, that part of you that has no beginning and no end?

Meditating upon these ideas, continue to gaze at the flame until your eyes become tired, then close them. You should see the candle-flame in front of your closed eyes. At first, it will probably dart around, eventually going out of focus. It is only with practice that we are able to keep it focused and still. If you meditate on a regular basis, a much brighter light, from the brow chakra itself, will appear before your closed eyes without the need for any external aid.

At the end of this meditation, bring your breathing back to normal, open your eyes and contemplate any insights it has brought you.

Blue

Blue is the dominant colour of the throat chakra and lies at the cold end of the spectrum. The endocrine gland associated with this chakra is the thyroid gland.

Blue symbolizes inspiration, devotion, peace and tranquillity. It is also a colour that creates a sense of space. As such, small rooms painted in this colour will appear to be larger. This property makes it an excellent colour to use for asthma, a breathing disorder characterized by a narrowing of the lungs' airways. Other diseases which respond beneficially to blue are stress, insomnia, high blood pressure and inflammation.

In the aura, a deep, clear blue represents pure religious feeling; a pale, ethereal blue indicates devotion to a noble idea; and bright blue suggests loyalty and sincerity. A dominance of blue in the aura signifies an artistic, harmonious nature and spiritual understanding.

On a physical level blue is associated with sadness and depression (which may have given rise to the expression 'feeling blue'). These associations suggest that blue should be used cautiously on people who are suffering from depressive conditions.

In many of the world's religions, blue is connected with deities. In Christianity it is the colour of the mantle worn by the Virgin Mary. There is speculation that the 'blue mantle' originally referred to the dominant colour displayed in her aura. In Greek and Roman pantheons blue represented the respected gods Jupiter and Zeus. In Hinduism, Krishna is shown as blue to illustrate that he is infinite.

The thyroid gland

The thyroid gland consists of two lobes, which are situated on either side of the trachea and joined together by an isthmus, which passes in front of the trachea. The main hormones secreted by this endocrine gland are thyroxine and triodothyronine. These contain a high percentage of iodine. One of the main functions of the thyroid gland is to restore iodine in the body. The thyroid's secretion of thyroxine is regulated by the thyroid-stimulating hormone (TSH) which is secreted by the anterior lobe of the pituitary gland.

The functions of the thyroid gland are:
- Controlling the metabolism of the body.
- Keeping the skin and hair in good condition.
- Cooperating with the other ductless glands to maintain the body's endocrine balance.
- Controlling body growth and mental development in infancy.
- Storing iodine.

The reflex to the thyroid gland is found just below the neck reflex, over the top half of the big toe. On the hand, it lies over the proximal phalanx of the thumb.

Reflexes Associated with the Colour Blue

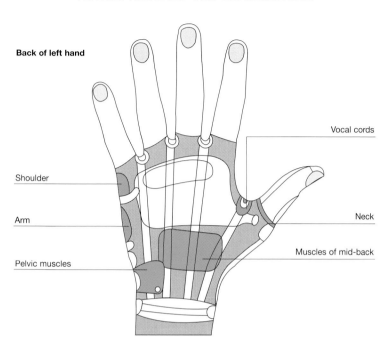

Back of left hand

Vocal cords

Shoulder

Arm

Pelvic muscles

Neck

Muscles of mid-back

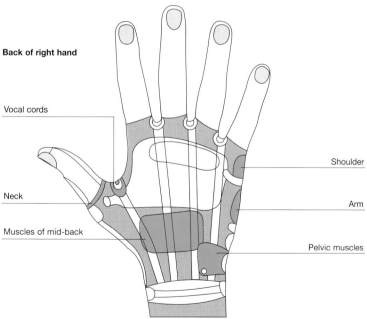

Back of right hand

Vocal cords

Neck

Muscles of mid-back

Shoulder

Arm

Pelvic muscles

REFLEXES ASSOCIATED WITH THE COLOUR BLUE

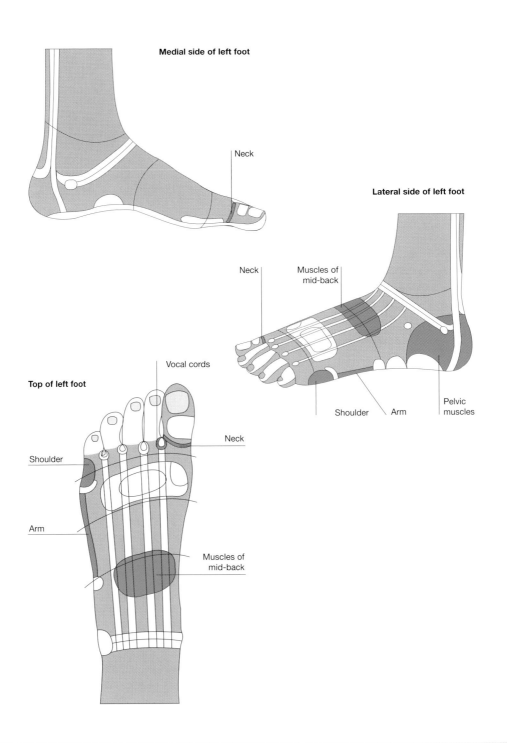

Medial side of left foot

Neck

Lateral side of left foot

Neck

Muscles of
mid-back

Shoulder

Arm

Pelvic
muscles

Top of left foot

Vocal cords

Neck

Shoulder

Arm

Muscles of
mid-back

Reflexes associated with the colour blue

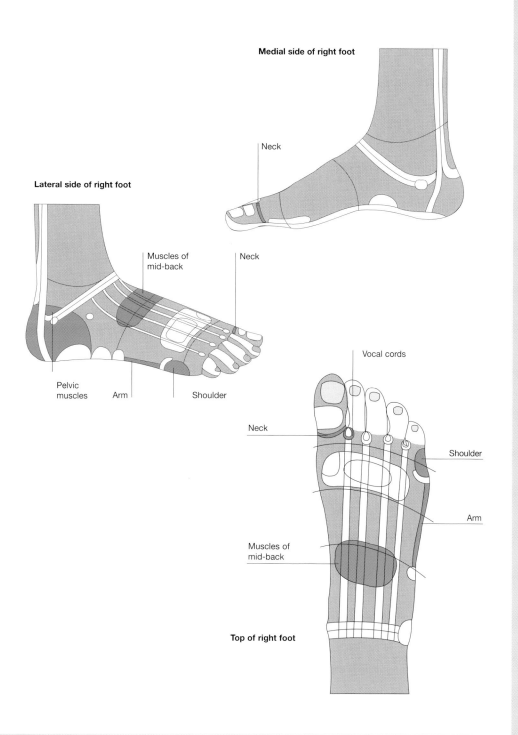

Medial side of right foot

Neck

Lateral side of right foot

Muscles of mid-back

Neck

Pelvic muscles

Arm

Shoulder

Vocal cords

Neck

Shoulder

Arm

Muscles of mid-back

Top of right foot

84

REFLEXES ASSOCIATED WITH THE COLOUR BLUE

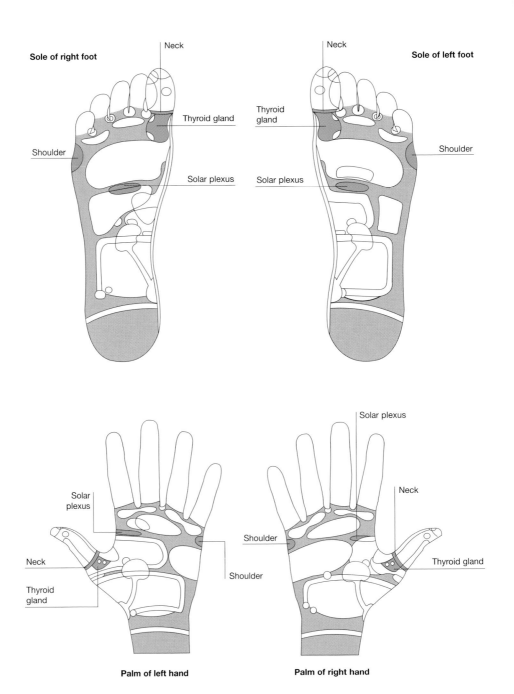

Sole of right foot

Neck

Thyroid gland

Shoulder

Solar plexus

Sole of left foot

Neck

Thyroid gland

Shoulder

Solar plexus

Solar plexus

Neck

Thyroid gland

Shoulder

Shoulder

Solar plexus

Neck

Shoulder

Thyroid gland

Palm of left hand

Palm of right hand

Associated Reflexes

Neck

The neck extends from the top of the chest to the base of the skull. Its main function is to support the head. The chief part of the neck is composed of seven cervical vertebrae (containing the cervical section of the spinal cord) and muscle.

The neck reflex is found around the base of the large toe, extending approximately one third up the distal aspect of this toe. On the hands it is located around the base of the thumb, extending approximately one third up the distal aspect of the thumb. My experience shows that the part of this reflex that extends up the distal aspect of the thumb or toe tends to be extremely painful in those suffering from neck problems.

Throat

The throat is a multi-purpose tube leading from the back of the nose and mouth down to the trachea (wind pipe) and oesophagus (food tube). Situated at the top of the trachea is the larynx.

The throat reflex forms part of the neck reflex and is treated alongside it.

Larynx

The larynx is the organ of voice. It houses stretched flaps of tissue – the vocal cords. When air passes over them they vibrate, producing sounds our mouth shapes into speech. The larynx is well protected by cartilage, one section of which, the thyroid cartilage, forms the Adam's Apple.

On the hands, the reflex for the vocal cords is located on the web between the thumb and index finger. On the feet it is found between the first and second toes.

Shoulders

The shoulder joint is formed by the upper end of the humerus and the shoulder blade. A loose, fibrous capsule, strengthened by ligamentous bands, surrounds the joint. Its main strength lies in its powerful muscles.

The shoulder reflex on the foot covers the lower part of the third phalanges and extends around the side of the toe to the front. On the hand, it lies around the base of the fifth finger, extending round the side of the finger to the back of the hand.

Solar plexus

The solar plexus comprises a large network of sympathetic nerves and ganglia situated in the abdomen, behind the stomach. Branches of the vagus nerve lead into the solar plexus where its branches are distributed to several abdominal organs.

On the feet and hands the solar plexus reflex lies under that of the diaphragm, in zones 2 and 3. On the feet it is positioned half way along the second and third metatarsals: on the hands it lies half way along the second and third metacarpals.

To be strictly correct, we would attribute yellow to this part of the body. The reason for including it here is because, in the majority of people, this is the place where nervous tension accumulates and is felt. I have always found it beneficial to use blue as a general colour on this reflex.

Treatment Colours
for Common Ailments

Thyroid gland

Thyrotoxicosis The word thyrotoxicosis means a poisoning of the body by the excess production of the hormone thyroxine. This is a condition that affects women more often than men. The symptoms are an increased metabolic rate, weight loss, intolerance to hot weather, emotional instability, frequent bowel action and an increase in heart rate.

To treat: Treatment colours are blue and orange to the thyroid reflex and gold and indigo to the pituitary reflex.

Hypothyroidism This is caused by a deficiency of thyroid hormones and can arise for a variety of reasons. The metabolic rate slows down inducing fatigue, lethargy, aching muscles, constipation and intolerance to cold. The body weight rises, despite dieting, and the skin becomes dry and puffy.

To treat: Treatment colours are orange and blue to the thyroid reflex and indigo and gold to the pituitary reflex.

NB: If a patient has been prescribed the drug thyroxine, his or her medical practitioner should monitor them throughout the course of reflexology and colour treatments. In the event of your treatment activating the thyroid gland to produce more thyroxine, the amount being taken synthetically may need to be reduced. If the thyroid gland has been surgically removed, there is no need for the patient to be monitored in this way.

Goitre This is a term applied to all swellings of the thyroid gland. There are many causes but most forms of generalized thyroid enlargement are due to a long-term excess of pituitary TSH in an attempt to stimulate the thyroid gland to proper functioning. Another cause is iodine deficiency.

To treat: Treatment colours are blue and orange to the thyroid reflex and indigo and gold to the pituitary reflex.

Neck

Stiff neck This can have many causes and should be investigated medically if it does not improve within three to four days. One simple cause is strain or injury to the neck muscles.

To treat: For this condition, treat the neck reflex with blue and its complementary orange.

Whiplash This injury is usually sustained in a car accident which causes the head to be suddenly thrown forward, and then jerked backwards, or vice versa. The main site of the injury is at the level of the fifth cervical vertebra where muscles and ligaments can be torn and strained.

To treat: If suffering from this complaint, it is advisable to seek help from a chiropractor immediately. Afterwards, the use of indigo and gold on the neck reflex is beneficial.

Throat

Sore throat Like the rest of the respiratory system, the throat is chiefly at risk from infection from a multitude of different bacteria or viruses. The most frequent cause of a sore throat is the common cold.

To treat: At the onset of the problem, treat the neck reflex with red/orange and turquoise.

Tonsillitis This is caused by germs attacking the tonsils and throat, both of which become painful and look redder than normal. There may also be a white coating over the tonsils.

To treat: As a first-aid treatment use red/orange and turquoise on the neck reflex.

Pharyngitis This is an inflammatory condition affecting the wall of the pharynx. It can be caused by either a bacterial or viral infestation. The symptoms are soreness, irritation and a tickling in the throat.

To treat: Treat the neck reflex with red/orange and turquoise.

Larynx

Laryngitis This is an inflammation of the larynx caused by an infection or by overuse or strain of the voice. It can also be associated with the common cold. The predominant symptom is hoarseness or complete loss of voice.

To treat: If the cause is an infection, use red/orange and turquoise on the vocal cord reflex. If brought on by over-use of the voice, use indigo and gold. It is also advisable for the patient to refrain from using his or her voice until the condition starts to improve.

Shoulders

Frozen shoulder The cause of this is unknown. There is no specific medical treatment but complete recovery normally occurs, although this may take some time. The symptoms are pain and stiffness in the shoulder, with considerable limitation of movement.

To treat: The treatment colours are indigo and gold to the shoulder reflex.

Bursitis Inflammation of the bursa (a sac containing lubricating fluid) that lies between the collarbone and the ball end of the upper arm bone. The inflammation is a result of injury to one of the structures lying in contact with the deep layer of the bursa. Chronic bursitis is due to too much movement of, or pressure on, a bursa, with fluid building up in the bursa.

To treat: Treatment colours are indigo and gold.

Arthritis and Rheumatism Arthritis is a word that describes actual inflammation in joints and their surrounding tissue. Rheumatic disease is a term used to describe disorders that cause pain and disability in joints, their supporting structures and connective tissues.

To treat: For pain associated with arthritis or rheumatism, work with indigo and gold on the shoulder reflex. For the actual condition, use yellow and violet. (These colours may be used on the reflexes of any other parts of the body suffering from either of these complaints.)

Reflex	Condition	Treatment Colour	Complementary Colour
Thyroid gland	Thyrotoxicosis		
	To pituitary reflex		
	Hypothyroidism		
	To pituitary reflex		
	Goitre		
	To pituitary reflex		
Neck	Stiff neck		
	Whiplash		
Throat	Sore throat		
	Tonsillitis		
	Pharyngitis		
Larynx	Laryngitis (infection)		
	Associated with strain		
Shoulders	Frozen shoulder		
	Bursitis		
	Arthritis & Rheumatism		
	Associated pain		

The Throat Chakra

The Sanskrit name for this chakra is 'Vishuddha', meaning 'to purify'. It is symbolized by a smoky violet-blue lotus flower with sixteen petals. In the centre of the lotus is a downward-pointing triangle containing a white circle. This chakra is associated with the element ether or *akasha* and the sense of hearing. The animal depicted is an elephant, the deities are Sadasiva and Sakini and the mantra or sound is 'ham'.

The throat centre represents a bridge leading from the physical to the spiritual realm. For this chakra to function to its full potential, the four lower elements, earth, water, fire and air, must be transmuted into the *akasha*. When we are spiritually ready for this to happen, our latent powers of telepathy, clairvoyance and clairaudience awaken. At this point in our evolution we must make sure not to be entrapped by these gifts: they could prevent us reaching our spiritual goal of self-realization.

In this chakra's awakened state, divine nectar (the mystical elixir of immortality) is tasted. This nectar is a sweet secretion produced by the lalana gland, located near the back of the throat. This nectar gland is stimulated by higher yogic practices and the nectar is purported to sustain a yogi for any length of time without food or water.

The throat chakra is the centre of creative intelligence and relates to the spoken word. It registers the creative purposes of the soul, transmitted to it by the inflow of energy from the brow centre. The fusion of these two energies leads to creative intelligence.

The use of this centre in communication is unique to humanity. In Tibetan mysticism, each sound is valued as a vibration, an invisible energy. This is the reason why Tibetan monks speak only at set times during the day and then only when necessary. Sound is also held sacred in Eastern mysticism. Sanskrit (the language in which most of the sacred texts of Hinduism were written) has fifty-two letters. These appear on the petals of the chakras and are intoned to awaken the chakra.

Today's endless, idle chatter and the constant bombardment of sound from our environment has deadened our sense of sound, especially our 'inner sense' of sound. A very therapeutic way of working with this chakra is singing. This for many is a forgotten pastime. Medieval Christian monastic infirmaries used music to help people in pain, to comfort the terminally ill and support a conscious death. Several years back, Theresa Schroedar-Sheker formed a group called the Chalice Midwives. They employed harp and voice in assisting the entire process of death and dying in home, hospital and hospice. Their work with pain resolution and the possibility of a conscious death is particularly attentive to the restoration of dignity, intimacy and reverence within the personal and community experience of death. Schroedar-Sheker describes this in her book *The Luminous Wand*.

On a physical level, this chakra governs the nervous system, female reproductive organs, the vocal cords, ears, shoulders, parathyroids and the thyroid gland. If this chakra becomes deficient in energy, it can make us timid, unreliable, manipulative, devious, inconsistent and afraid of sex. If it is over-stimulated a person can become arrogant, an excessive talker, dogmatic and self-righteous. Balanced energy here makes us contented, centred and a good speaker. We can be musically or artistically inspired and have no difficulty living in the present.

Some of the physical symptoms that can arise from an imbalanced throat chakra are eye problems, headaches, hormonal imbalances, sleeplessness, migraine, sinus problems, hay fever and catarrh.

The throat chakra reflex on the feet and hands

On the feet, the throat chakra is located approximately a third of the way along the second phalanx of the big toe: on the hand it is situated approximately half way along the second phalanx of the thumb. To check for imbalances, place your finger on the chakra's reflex on either the foot or the hand. Now, with your pendulum, dowse to ascertain if this chakra is in balance, or to find out if it is under-active (deficient in energy) or over-active (contains too much energy). If it is under-active, treat with blue; and if it is over-active, treat with orange.

To treat, either use the reflexology torch or place your finger on the reflex point and channel the required colour.

THE POSITION OF THE THROAT CHAKRA REFLEX ON THE FEET AND HANDS

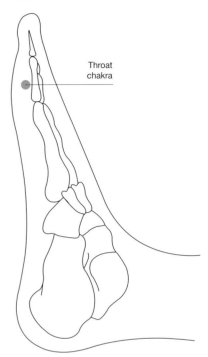

Throat chakra

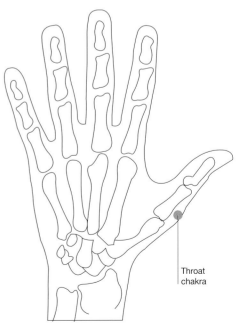

Throat chakra

Visualization with Blue

It is a pleasantly warm day in spring and you are walking through a wood carpeted with bluebells. Finding a fallen tree trunk, sit down and observe this spectacle of colour. Notice how wonderfully and intricately these flowers are made. Each tiny bell possesses its own individuality of colour and shape.

Closing your eyes and visualizing one of these flowers, you find that its bell shape starts to expand until it completely surrounds you and you find yourself sitting inside it. The stamens provide a pillow upon which to rest your head. Lie back and feel the softness of the petals encircling you like a soft mantle. The blue rays emanating from the petals play upon your body, releasing tension and stress. Your inhalation and exhalation deepens as your body relaxes. As you inhale, you breathe this colour into your body through all the pores in your skin. Where there is bodily discomfort, visualize the colour surrounding the affected part, bringing relaxation and healing.

You begin to feel a deep sense of peace and tranquillity. You lose all sense of time and place and start to become part of the peace surrounding you. Your physical body melts into this atmosphere of tranquillity and you start to sense your higher self, a feeling unique to each of us. You become conscious that it is inviting you to lay before it any worries or problems you may have. As you accept this invitation, you know that, when the time is right, answers to these problems will be given – through your intuition, through a friend, or perhaps through a book that you are reading.

As you end this visualization by increasing your inhalation and exhalation, the flower of the bluebell starts to shrink and you become aware of your body sitting in your chosen place. Open your eyes and reflect on your experience.

Meditation with the Throat Chakra

Our throat chakra is our centre of creativity, of sound and of the spoken word. Everything that exists as part of our universe vibrates to its own unique sound. Because we are a microcosm of the macrocosm we too vibrate to harmonic sounds. These subtle sounds can be heard only with our inner sense of hearing, in meditative silence. Unfortunately, many of us have lost the art of listening in this way, and to recover it takes practice.

Sitting comfortably in a place free from external noise, begin this meditation by concentrating on your breath. Slowly breathe in and out to a count of five. This will help induce a state of relaxation in both body and mind. If you find your thoughts start to wander, gently bring them back to your breath.

When you are relaxed, allow your breath to resume its normal rhythm. Now concentrate on your throat chakra. Visualize this as a smoky blue lotus flower floating on a calm pool of water. Imagine this flower growing in size until it is large enough for you to sit at its centre. Looking around, you notice a frog sitting quietly on one of the flower's leaves; a collection of fish swimming beneath the waters surface; an assortment of variegated coloured stones scattered around the pool's edge. Beyond the pool lie fields, and trees whose leaves rustle softly in the gentle breeze. Animals graze on the lush green grass, some sheltering beneath the trees' overhanging branches, away from the heat of the midday sun.

Observing this scene, listen for the outward sounds made by the animals, the rustling leaves and the call of birds flying overhead. As you register each sound, stay with it until it becomes inaudible. Now 'tune in' to your inner sense of hearing and listen for any sounds coming from the stones, the grass, the fish and the lotus upon which you are sitting. Lastly, rest your concentration on your own body and listen for its undulating harmony.

End the meditation by increasing your inhalation and exhalation. Then open your eyes and spend a few moments reflecting on your experiences. If no sounds were audible to your 'inner sense of hearing', don't be discouraged. With practice and patience this will happen for you.

Green

The colour green lies at the centre of the colour spectrum and is linked with a sense of balance in all aspects of oneself. As the colour of balance it is able to bring stability to both mind and emotions. It is very restful on the eyes because it is focused almost exactly on to the retina by the eye's lens. As such it could be a valuable colour for those working long hours at a computer or under artificial light.

In nature, green is both the colour of life found in the new foliage of spring, and the colour of decay, as mould on rotting vegetation. Being the colour of nature it is reputed to cool the blood and animate the nervous system. Often, a walk through green fields or among a forest's green foliage will soothe, calm and relax.

Being the dominant colour of the heart chakra and the colour given to the planet Venus, green is also associated with love. It was a colour traditionally worn at weddings in Europe, where it symbolized fertility.

The negative aspects of green are jealousy, nausea, poison and envy. When the body is diseased it produces unpleasant greens in the form of pus and phlegm.

In the aura, bright, clear greens symbolize good qualities; light greens, prosperity and success; mid-green, adaptability and versatility; clear green, sympathy; dark green, deceit; olive green, treachery and double nature. An abundance of green denotes individualism and independence.

Lime green, formed by mixing green with yellow, is used to counteract toxicity in the body. This is a good colour to use on the liver reflex for anyone taking medically prescribed drugs or on a diet high in coffee and junk food. This colour can be administered through the throat chakra to cleanse the bloodstream and the etheric layer of the aura from stagnant energy.

The thymus gland

The thymus is the endocrine gland associated with the heart chakra, but the colour it vibrates to is turquoise. Because of its connection with the heart chakra, I am including it in this section, but its association with the lymphatic system means that turquoise should be used as the general colour. Information on turquoise is given on pages 154–159.

The thymus gland is situated in the thorax, behind the sternum and in front of the heart. It consists mainly of lymphoid tissue and plays a part in the formation of lymphocytes. At birth, this gland is quite large: it continues to increase in size until puberty, when it starts to get smaller. The thymus plays an important part in the body's immune system.

It is claimed that certain yogic practices can keep this gland active, thereby keeping a person youthful and the immune system strong.

The thymus reflex is located on the back of the hands, over the medial half of the ball of the thumb. On the feet it is found on the medial side of the big toes, covering the second phalanx.

REFLEXES ASSOCIATED WITH THE COLOUR GREEN

Sole of right foot

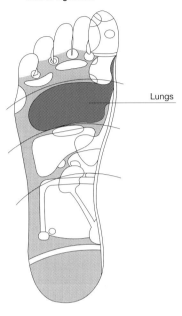

Lungs

Sole of left foot

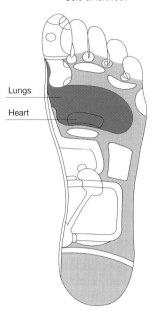

Lungs

Heart

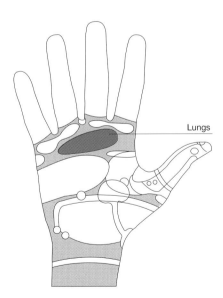

Palm of right hand

Lungs

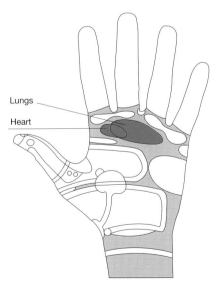

Lungs

Heart

Palm of left hand

REFLEXES ASSOCIATED WITH THE COLOUR GREEN

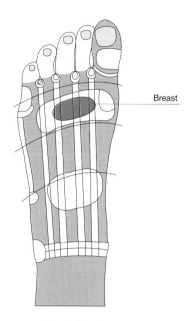

Breast

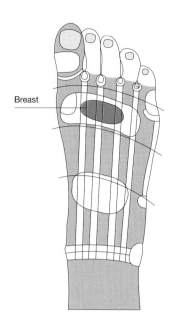

Breast

Top of left foot

Top of right foot

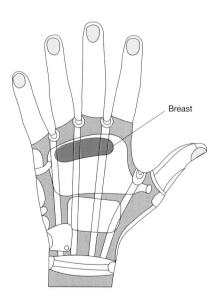

Breast

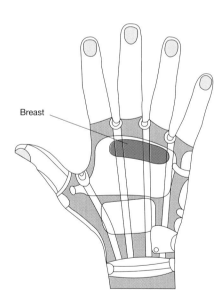

Breast

Back of left hand

Back of right hand

Associated Reflexes

Lungs

The two lungs, situated side by side in the chest cavity, are conical in shape and greyish in colour, each lung being encased in a thin membrane, the pleura. The right lung has three lobes; the left lung, which is slightly smaller, has two. A deep fissure divides each lobe. Each lung is filled with air sacs called alveoli and through these the exchange of gases takes place.

When we breathe, air is drawn in through the nose where it is warmed and moistened. On its journey to the lungs it passes down the first section of the oesophagus (food tube) and into the larynx. To prevent solids and liquids from entering, the larynx is guarded by the epiglottis, a leaf-like piece of cartilage covered with mucous membrane. The air then passes into the trachea (a continuation of the larynx) which divides into two bronchi, one going to the left lung and the other to the right. The bronchi then divide and sub-divide into smaller air tubes that resemble an inverted tree. The smallest tubes, the bronchioles, terminate in air sacs or alveoli. Into these the inhaled air finally passes. An exchange of gases takes place through the alveoli's thin walls. Oxygen is taken up by the blood vessels, while carbon dioxide and other waste products are passed back into the alveoli to be exhaled.

The reflex for the right lung is located on the sole of the right foot and the palm of the right hand; the reflex for the left lung is on the sole of the left foot and the palm of the left hand. These reflexes cover zones 1 to 5 and lie between the shoulder girdle and the diaphragm.

Heart

The heart is a cone-shaped, muscular organ about the size of a clenched fist. It lies within a strong fibrous bag, the pericardium. The heart is situated roughly in the centre of the chest – two thirds of it to the left of the sternum (breast bone), and the other third to the right. The heart is divided centrally by a solid muscular wall, the septum. This prevents blood in the two sides of the heart from mixing.

Each side of the heart has two hollow chambers: the atrium at the top and the ventricle below. A valve guards the opening between each atrium and ventricle to prevent the back-flow of blood. The right side of the heart receives de-oxygenated blood which it pumps to the lungs to expel carbon dioxide and pick up oxygen from inhaled air: the left side

THE HEART

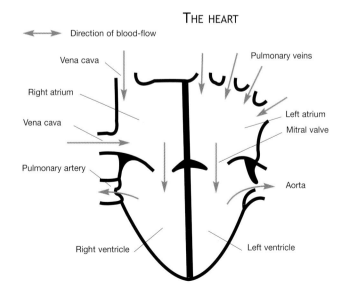

Direction of blood-flow

Vena cava

Right atrium

Vena cava

Pulmonary artery

Right ventricle

Pulmonary veins

Left atrium

Mitral valve

Aorta

Left ventricle

Treating cancer

In my work as a colour practitioner I have treated a number of people with cancer. As a life-threatening disease, all types of cancer should be treated only by qualified practitioners.

Several years ago, I attended a course, organized by the Lynda Jackson Center and held at Mount Vernon Hospital, for complementary practitioners working with cancer patients. I found this very informative and would recommend it to anyone working in the complementary field. For further information on these courses you need to contact the Lynda Jackson Center whose address is given at the back of the book. Following this course I worked in palliative care and found that using colour with reflexology was beneficial both physically and emotionally for the patients I treated.

If the person attending for treatment is still awaiting surgery, I would recommend that magenta and its complementary lime green be applied to the appropriate reflex. For example, if the patient is suffering breast cancer, then colour would be applied through the breast reflex on either the left or right foot.

If the tumour has been surgically removed, then yellow with its complementary violet would be applied to the reflex to help the scar tissue.

If the person has, or is suspected of having, secondary tumours, then both feet are flooded with magenta with its complementary lime green.

If the patient is having chemotherapy or radium treatment then care needs to be taken because with chemotherapy the body becomes very toxic and with radium treatment the tissues surrounding the site where the radium is given can become sore. This care applies to reflexology and the integration of colour with reflexology.

For terminally ill patients it is preferable to channel the required colours through your hands rather than use the reflexology crystal torch. This allows the paler shades of colour to be used.

receives re-oxygenated blood from the lungs which it pumps to the body via a vast network of vessels.

Blood from the veins of the head, neck and upper limbs enters the right atrium through the superior vena cava; blood from the rest of the body and lower limbs enters by the inferior vena cava. The blood then passes through the tricuspid valve into the right ventricle: it leaves the right ventricle through the pulmonary artery to pass to the capillaries of the lungs. Here the pulmonary veins collect it and carry it to the left atrium. It then passes through the mitral valve to the left ventricle and leaves by the aorta, the body's large main artery.

The heart reflex is located on the sole of the left foot and palm of the left hand, just above the diaphragm in zones 2 and 3.

Breasts

Each breast, or mammary gland, consists of approximately fifteen to twenty groups of milk-producing glands embedded in fatty tissue. On the surface of each breast is a central pink disc called the areola, which surrounds the nipple and contains small sebaceous glands that keep it supple.

The breast enlargement that occurs in pregnancy is due to development of the glands in preparation for lactation.

The breast reflex is located above the diaphragm, in zones 2, 3 and 4, on the top of both feet and back of both hands.

Treatment Colours for Common Ailments

Lungs

Asthma This is characterized by recurring spasms of the smooth muscle in the walls of the bronchial air passages. The muscle contractions narrow the airways making breathing difficult. Excessive mucus can accompany this condition, causing further airway obstruction. Asthma attacks can be triggered by stress, infection or inhaling allergens or other irritants.

To treat: Treatment colours are blue with its complementary orange to the lung reflex.

Acute bronchitis A condition characterized by acute inflammation of the bronchi, acute bronchitis is most commonly caused by infection originating in the upper part of the respiratory track. The illness usually starts with a non-productive cough that develops to produce mucus containing pus.

To treat: Treatment colours are orange with its complementary blue to the lung reflex.

Pneumonia An acute inflammation of the lungs in which the bronchi and tiny air sacs (alveoli) become covered with a thick fluid. Pneumonia is usually the result of a bacterial infection, but may be caused by viruses and fungi. Symptoms are headache, cough, chest pain and a high fever.

To treat: Treatment colours are red/orange with its complementary turquoise to the lung reflex.

Lung cancer Lung cancer affects the pulmonary tissue and destroys the lungs' vital gas-exchange function. The medical profession reports that cigarette smoking causes about 75 per cent of lung cancers. Other possible factors are 'passive smoking', asbestos, chromium, coal products and ionising radiation.

To treat: Treatment colours are magenta and lime green to the lung reflex. (See also Treating Cancer, page 98.)

Heart

Angina This describes the severe chest pain that occurs when the heart muscle is deprived of an adequate amount of oxygen.

To treat: Treatment colours are indigo and its complementary gold to the heart reflex.

Tachycardia This is characterized by a rapid heart rhythm. Although normal during and after exercise, other, more worrisome causes are stress, blood loss, shock, drugs and fever.

To treat: When caused by stress the treatment colours are blue and its complementary orange on the heart reflex.

Extrosystoles This is a condition where premature contraction of one or more chambers of the heart occurs. A beat of the heart occurs sooner than it should and is followed by a longer rest than usual before the next beat. The cause can be prolonged stress.

To treat: Treatment colours are orange with its complementary blue to the heart reflex.

Palpitations Characterized by a forceful or irregular heart beat, palpitations can be caused by a sudden fright, stress, or an over indulgence in tobacco, tea, coffee or alcohol.
To treat: Treatment colours are blue with its complementary orange to the heart reflex.

A 'broken heart' This stems from deep emotional pain. The colours used for heartbreak are not complementary to each other but are very effective. Violet has the power to mend the broken heart and restore dignity and self respect; rose pink fills with unconditional love the void that is often left.
To treat: Treatment colours are violet and rose pink.

Breasts

Breast abscess Otherwise known as mastitis, this is an infected area of tissue formed when microbes enter the breast tissue through the nipple or through a break in the skin. Symptoms are a red, tender swelling or lump in the breast, possibly a raised temperature, and tender glands in the armpit next to the infected breast.
To treat: Treatment colours are red/orange and its complementary turquoise to the breast reflex.

Breast cyst Cysts are fluid-filled sacs of tissue. They are usually benign, but if a patient finds any lump in the breast he or she should report it to their general practitioner immediately.

To treat: Treatment colours are magenta and its complementary lime green to the breast reflex.

Breast cancer This is a malignant tumour. When the tumour measures approximately 2.5 centimetres/1 inch across, it may start to spread, via the blood stream and the upper lymphatic system, to other parts of the body. Early medical diagnosis is absolutely vital.
To treat: Treatment colours are magenta and its complementary lime green to the breast reflex. (See Treating Cancer, page 98.) Treat scar tissue with yellow and violet.

Lactation Soon after the birth of a baby the hormone prolactin, secreted by the pituitary gland, stimulates the breasts to start secreting milk. Occasionally, lactation does not occur. A midwife, attending one of my courses, advised her non-lactating mothers to imagine that they were sitting beneath an orange waterfall. Mothers using this visualization very soon started to lactate (see below).
To treat: Use orange with its complementary blue on the pituitary reflex, and encourage the patient to work with the following visualization.

Imagine yourself sitting on a boulder beneath a gentle waterfall on a sunny summer's day. Visualize the water turning a clear orange as it gently flows over your head, down your body and into the surrounding earth. As the colour's vibrational energy enters through your eyes and the pores of your skin, envisage it interacting with your pituitary gland in your head, to encourage it to secrete the hormone that stimulates lactation.

Reflex	Condition	Treatment Colour	Complementary Colour
Lungs	Asthma		
	Acute bronchitis		
	Pneumonia		
	Cancer		
Heart	Angina		
	Tachycardia		
	Extrosystoles		
	Palpitations		
	'Broken heart'		
Breasts	Abscess		
	Cyst		
	Cancer		
	For scar tissue		
	Lactation		
	To the pituitary reflex		

The **Heart Chakra**

The word 'anahata' means 'the unstruck'. All sound in the universe is produced by striking together objects, thus setting up vibrations or sound waves. The primordial sound which comes from beyond this universe is the source of all sound and is known as the anahata sound.

The sound we perceive with our ears is only one level of perception. If sound waves exist at a conscious level they must also exist at subtler levels. The ancient Rishis and yogis who had contacted the deeper levels of the mind through meditation, perceived the sounds of these subtler vibrations. They discovered that the sound of the ingoing and outgoing breath was the link between the individual consciousness and cosmic consciousness.

The heart chakra is situated between the fourth and fifth thoracic vertebrae and is symbolized by twelve green petals. Inside the petals is a circle containing a smoky blue hexagram constructed from an upward- and a downward-pointing triangle. The downward-pointing triangle is associated with the lower nature of humankind and the earth energies. The upward-pointing triangle stands for humankind's higher nature and is linked to our spiritual energies. The animal depicted is the antelope and the mantra or sound this chakra resonates to is YAM. Anahata is associated with the element air and the sense of touch.

This is the centre where we experience love, and through it we connect with those with whom we have a love relationship. Love can be expressed on many levels. It can be purely selfish, demanding and constricting, or it can be compassionate and caring. The more open this centre is, the greater our capacity to extend undemanding, spiritual love. When anahata awakens, it brings greater sensitivity to the sense of touch and a detachment from material objects.

When anahata's energies are balanced, compassion is generated: we have a desire to nurture others and we aspire towards unconditional love. People thus balanced are in touch with their feelings and are outgoing, friendly and compassionate. Excessive energy in this chakra can produce depression, moodiness and possessiveness: it can make a person demanding and a master of conditional love. If the chakra is deficient in energy it can create paranoia, indecisiveness, a desire to hang on to objects or people, a need for constant reassurance and a fear of being rejected and hurt.

Physically, this chakra is associated with the heart and circulatory system, the immune system and the lungs. The endocrine gland attributed to it is the thymus. The physical symptoms that can arise through a malfunctioning heart chakra are high blood pressure, heart disease, breathing problems, lung disease and asthma.

Situated just below the heart chakra is a smaller centre represented by a lotus flower with eight red petals. This chakra is known as the ananda-kanda or kalpa tree. Inside the lotus flower is the tree of life and an altar sparkling with many precious gems, the seat of the true self.

The heart chakra reflex on the feet and hands

The reflex for this chakra is found at the top of the first metatarsal bone on the feet and on the hands it is at the point where the second phalanx meets the first metacarpal bone. To find out if this chakra is in balance, place your finger on the reflex point for this chakra on either the hand or the foot and with your other hand use your pendulum to dowse. If you find the chakra is over-active treat with a pale shade of red, if it is under-active treat with green.

To treat, use either the reflexology torch or place your finger on the reflex point and channel the required colour through yourself.

THE POSITION OF THE HEART CHAKRA REFLEX ON THE HANDS AND FEET

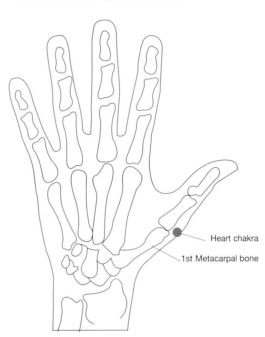

Heart chakra

1st Metacarpal bone

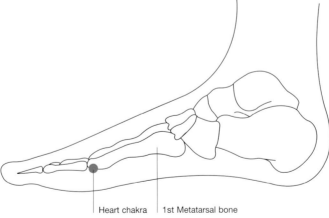

Heart chakra   1st Metatarsal bone

Visualization with Green

Imagine that you are standing at the entrance to a corridor. Notice how rough and uneven the natural stone walls are and observe the various shapes and sizes of the cobble-stones on the floor. Looking down the corridor you see an old, oval-shaped, wooden door with rusty hinges and a circular, rusty iron handle.

Walk down the corridor towards the door and, when you reach it, turn the handle, push the door open and walk through into the spacious circular room that lies beyond. This room is filled with shafts of light in every conceivable shade of green and no sound disturbs its breathless quietude. Looking up to the centre of the ceiling, you observe that the source of the green light is a large, faceted emerald.

Slowly walk around the room's perimeter, and as you pass through each shade of green be conscious of how it is affecting you physically and emotionally. Be mindful of the shade that you feel drawn towards, and whether you have chosen it for its therapeutic or cosmetic value.

When you have passed through all the shades of green, move to the centre of the room where there is a shallow pond with pale pink water lilies floating on its surface. Around the edge of the pond are large white cushions. Lie down on one of these and look up at the emerald stone and the pale pink diaphanous aura that surrounds it. Feel the energy that pulsates from its heart. Imagine a ray of green light emanating from this stone, flooding your body with the shade you were attracted to.

As you relax in this colour, it soothes and refreshes your eyes; it releases tension and restores balance to your heart, lungs, breasts and all the muscles surrounding the upper part of the trunk of your body. Green is the colour of nature and produces a soothing, harmonious radiation that is essential for our well-being.

When you feel ready, end this visualization by contemplating what you have experienced. Try to spend some time each week amidst the greens of nature.

Meditation with the Heart Chakra

Imagine that you are walking through a forest on a path carpeted with fallen leaves and twigs in their various stages of decay. The protruding roots of the majestically towering trees make their own intricate design upon the earth, and the trees' branches, as they stretch towards the light of the sun, intertwine to form a vaulted roof for what you realize is one of nature's living cathedrals. The air around you is damp from its prolonged lack of sunshine and the only noise is the crackling and rustling sound made by the twigs and leaves as you walk over them.

Lying down in a comfortable, dry niche, shaped from the trees' roots, observe the varying shades of green fashioned by the interplay of shadow and light. On your next inhalation, visualize a ray of clear green light entering your heart chakra.

The heart chakra is our centre of balance and union of opposites. This is symbolized by the upward-pointing and downward-pointing triangles that form the Star of David, the geometric sign present here. If we were to draw a vertical line down the centre of our body, separating our left and right sides, and a horizontal line through the heart chakra to separate the three lower and three upper chakras, we would create an equal-limbed cross symbolizing our physical, mental, emotional and spiritual attributes. It is these aspects of ourself that become integrated at the heart centre through the power of unconditional love.

As the ray of green light enters your heart chakra, allow it to bring to balance the left and right hemispheres of your brain, your masculine and feminine energies and your three upper and lower chakras. Whilst doing this, bring your inhalation and exhalation into balance by making your in-breath the same length as your out-breath. Then relax and enjoy the scene you have created.

End this meditation by contemplating any insights it has brought you.

Yellow

Yellow's sunny disposition radiates warmth and inspiration, making it the happiest of colours.

In relation to other primaries in the colour spectrum, yellow occupies a comparatively narrow band, but it has the highest reflectivity of all the colours. Its positive magnetic currents are both stimulating and inspiring, making it beneficial for skin problems, and arthritic and rheumatic conditions. Yellow clears the nervous system of stagnant energy when applied to the brow chakra, head and spine.

In food, especially fruit, it signifies the presence of iron and the vitamins A and C. Spectroscopically, yellow is found in all herbs which are purgative, such as senna, or are nerve stimulants. It is also a colour that helps the body to metabolize calcium, perhaps because of its closeness to sunlight (sunlight produces vitamin D in the body, an essential vitamin for calcium metabolism). As a result, yellow is useful for treating osteoporosis and calcium deficiencies.

Yellow is the dominant colour of the solar plexus chakra. In the aura, golden yellow denotes high soul qualities, a pale primrose indicates great intellectual power, a dark, dingy yellow suggests jealousy and suspicion, and a dull, lifeless yellow relates to false optimism. An excess of yellow in the aura indicates an abundance of mental power.

Because yellow works with the intellect and mental inspiration, it is good to use, in small quantities, in places of learning. However, to be completely surrounded by yellow for a long period of time could cause a state of mental and emotional detachment. This makes it an inadvisable colour to use with those suffering from mental disorders.

Yellow's negative attributes are connected with cowardice. This association could have arisen from a practice of sixteenth-century Spain, where people found guilty of heresy and treason were made to wear yellow before being burnt at the stake.

The pancreas (islets of langerhans)

The pancreas is similar in structure to the salivary glands. It is a long, thin gland that lies transversely behind the stomach. It has two major functions. The first is to produce enzymes, which flow through the pancreatic duct into the duodenum where they help to digest food. The second function is to produce, using the microscopic cells known as the islets of langerhans, the hormones insulin and glucagons. These microscopic cells are the endocrine part of the pancreas and are associated with the solar plexus chakra.
This reflex is found on the soles of both feet and the palms of both hands. On both the feet and hands it is situated below the diaphragm and extends to just above the waist line. On the left foot and hand it covers zones 1, 2 and 3 and on the right foot and hand it covers zones 1 and 2.

REFLEXES ASSOCIATED WITH THE COLOUR YELLOW

Sole of right foot

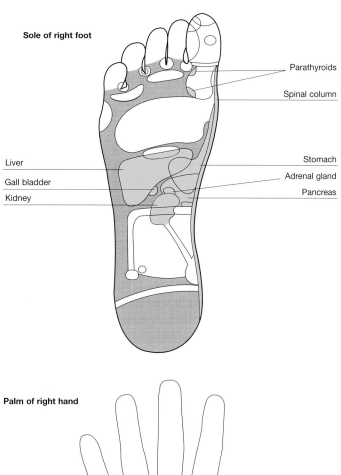

Parathyroids

Spinal column

Liver

Gall bladder

Kidney

Stomach

Adrenal gland

Pancreas

Palm of right hand

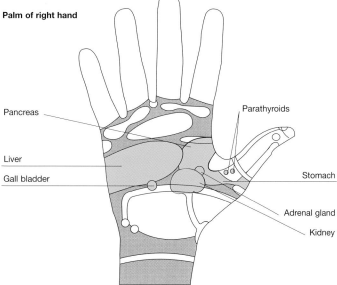

Pancreas

Parathyroids

Liver

Gall bladder

Stomach

Adrenal gland

Kidney

REFLEXES ASSOCIATED WITH THE COLOUR YELLOW

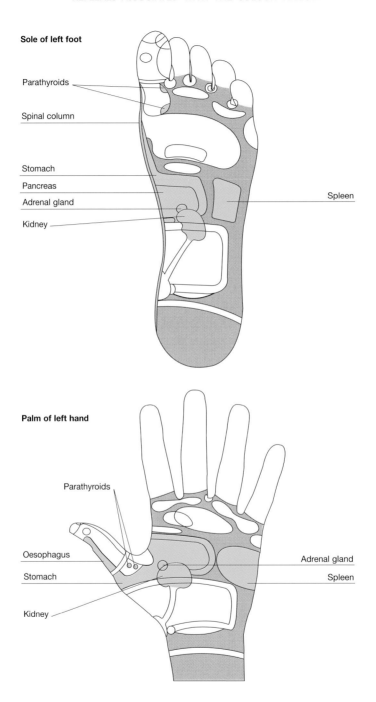

Sole of left foot

Parathyroids

Spinal column

Stomach

Pancreas

Adrenal gland

Kidney

Spleen

Palm of left hand

Parathyroids

Oesophagus

Stomach

Kidney

Adrenal gland

Spleen

REFLEXES ASSOCIATED WITH THE COLOUR YELLOW

Back of left hand

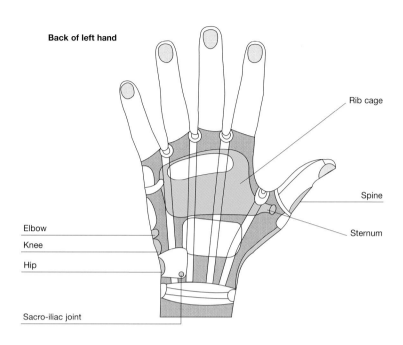

Rib cage

Spine

Sternum

Elbow

Knee

Hip

Sacro-iliac joint

Back of right hand

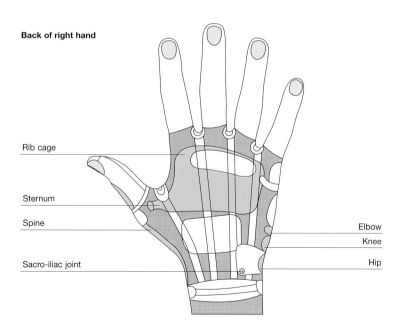

Rib cage

Sternum

Spine

Sacro-iliac joint

Elbow

Knee

Hip

REFLEXES ASSOCIATED WITH THE COLOUR YELLOW

Top of left foot

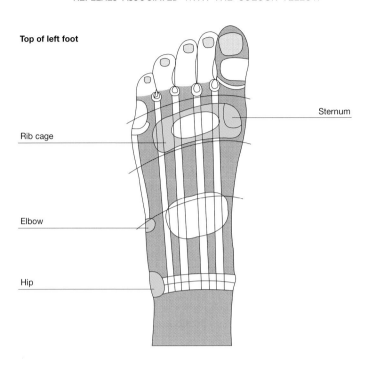

Sternum

Rib cage

Elbow

Hip

Top of right foot

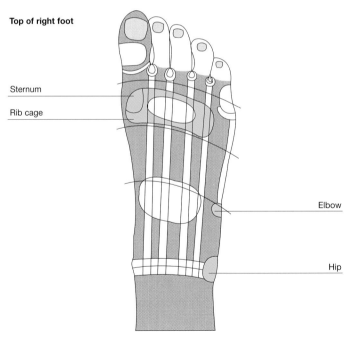

Sternum

Rib cage

Elbow

Hip

REFLEXES ASSOCIATED WITH THE COLOUR YELLOW

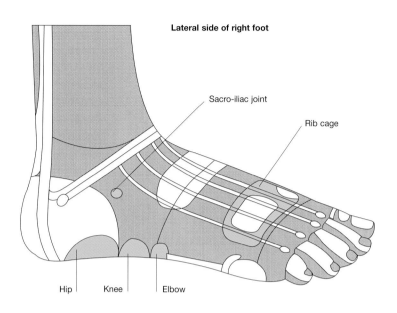

Lateral side of right foot

Sacro-iliac joint

Rib cage

Hip Knee Elbow

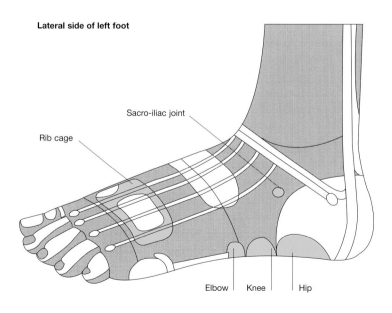

Lateral side of left foot

Rib cage

Sacro-iliac joint

Elbow Knee Hip

Associated Reflexes

THE HUMAN SKELETON

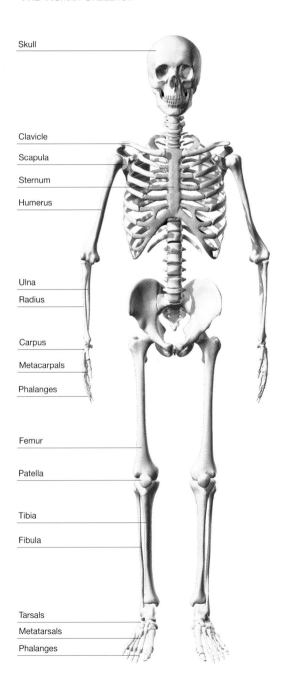

Skull

Clavicle

Scapula

Sternum

Humerus

Ulna

Radius

Carpus

Metacarpals

Phalanges

Femur

Patella

Tibia

Fibula

Tarsals

Metatarsals

Phalanges

Nervous system

Put simply, the nervous system consists of two principle divisions. One is the central nervous system, so called because the brain and the spinal cord, of which it consists, occupy a central location in the body. The other is the peripheral nervous system, which is constituted by the nerves connecting the brain and spinal cord to other parts of the body: its sub-division, the autonomic nervous system, is responsible for regulating the body's automatic or involuntary functions, such as the heart rate.

The nervous system is connected to the *nadis* found in the etheric layer of the aura. The general colour given to the nervous system is yellow because this is the colour nearest to sunlight.

Skeletal system

The average human skeleton consists of approximately 206 bones. In some people this number can vary slightly from the norm. In the male skeleton the bones are a little larger and heavier than in the female and the pelvic cavity is narrower. The bones of the skeleton are connected by joints. These comprise freely mobile joints that provide flexibility in movement, fixed joints which hold bones firmly together, as in the skull, and partially mobile joints which allow some flexibility in movement.

The parts of the skeleton described in this section are the ones directly related to reflex points found on the feet and the hands.

Spine or vertebral column

For a description of the spine, see page 22. An important feature of the spinal column is the presence of four curves. These occur within the cervical vertebrae, the thoracic vertebrae, the lumbar spine and the sacrum and coccyx. These curves serve to minimize jolting and jarring of the internal organs. The vertebrae are linked by strong ligaments and have flexible discs lying between them – discs which provide a certain amount of elasticity, to permit movement of the spine. Throughout the length of the spine is a channel through which the spinal cord passes: side channels allow peripheral nerves to pass to and from the rest of the body.

This reflex is found on both feet. It starts on the medial border of the big toe (the cervical spine) and continues along the medial side of the foot, just below the arch, to two thirds of the way along the calcaneum. On the hands it is situated along the medial border of the thumb ending where the scaphoid bone joins the radius.

Sternum

The sternum or breast bone is flat, and to it are attached the costal cartilages of the ribs.

This reflex is found on the top of both feet and the back of both hands. On the feet it is located below the base of the big toe in zone 1 and on the hands it is situated in zone 1, on the medial edge of the metacarpal bone head.

Rib cage

The rib cage contains twelve pairs of ribs. These are flat, curved bars of bone which are attached posteriorly to the spinal vertebrae. The upper seven pairs are attached to the sternum, at the front of the body, by costal cartilage and bear the name 'true ribs'. The eighth, ninth and tenth pairs of ribs are attached, at the front of the body, to the cartilage of the seventh pair of ribs. The eleventh and twelfth pairs of ribs are not attached to the front of the body, and are known as 'floating ribs'. The ribs, sternum and thoracic vertebrae of the spine form the bony cage that houses the organs of the chest.

This reflex is located on the upper part of the front of the feet and hands. It covers all five zones on each foot and hand.

Elbow

The elbow joint is formed between the humerus bone in the upper part of the arm and the radius and ulna bones in the lower part. The joint is secured at the sides by strong lateral ligaments, and both the back and front of the joint are covered by powerful muscles.

The reflex area to the elbow joint is found at the outer edge of the left and the right foot, at the base of the fifth metatarsal bone; on the left and right hand it is at the base of the fifth metacarpal bone.

Knee

The knee is formed by the femur, tibia and patella, or knee cap, and it is the largest hinge joint in the body. The cavity of the knee joint is intricate and the ligaments that bind the bones together are very strong.

This reflex is located on the outer border of both feet and hands. On the feet it is found behind the bony projection of the fifth metatarsals, and on the hands it can be found just below the waist line.

Hip

The hip joint is of the ball-and-socket variety and is formed by the head of the thigh bone and the deep, cup-shaped hollow on the side of the pelvis, into which it fits. The joint is enclosed by a capsule of fibrous tissue and strengthened by several bands of ligaments.

The reflex to the hip is moon shaped and is found on the outer side of both feet and hands, directly behind the knee reflex. On the foot it extends to the back of the heel and on the hand it extends to the wrist.

Sacro-iliac joint

The sacro-iliac joint is where the sacrum of the spine meets the ileum of the pelvis. It is a joint with very little movement. Its importance lies in its transmission of body weight through the vertebral column, via the pelvis, to the lower limbs.

The reflex is found in the dip which lies just in front of each ankle bone. On the back of each hand it lies just above the wrist, between zones 4 and 5.

Parathyroids

These four small glands, each about the size of a pea, are situated in the neck, one behind each of the four corners of the thyroid gland. These glands secrete a hormone called parathormone which controls the body's calcium metabolism.

The reflexes are found on the soles of the feet and palms of the hands at the top and base of the lateral edge of the thyroid gland.

Liver

The liver is the largest, solid organ of the body: it is located mainly on the right side, beneath the diaphragm. It is divided by a fissure into a large right lobe and a smaller left lobe. The liver comprises a large number of lobules, each consisting of columns of liver cells. From each lobule passes a small bile duct which carries the cells' bile secretions. These small bile ducts then join with similar ducts from other lobules to form larger bile ducts.

In addition to forming bile, the liver has many important functions. Among these are storage of the iron and copper necessary for the manufacture of red corpuscles, storage of carbohydrates in the form of glycogen, the formation of vitamin A from carotene, and the storage of B vitamins. The liver also plays an essential role in the storage and metabolism of fat.

The liver reflex is found only on the sole of the right foot and palm of the right hand. It is located beneath the diaphragm and just above the waist line. Beneath the diaphragm, where the reflex begins, it covers zones 1, 2 and 3, gradually diminishing in size to cover zones 1 and 2 at its finishing point above the waist line.

Gall bladder

The gall bladder is a pear-shaped sac situated on the under surface of the liver's right lobe. It acts as a reservoir for storing bile. During its stay in the gall bladder, the bile is concentrated by the extraction of water. After a meal, especially if it contains fat, the gall bladder contracts and sends the bile via the cystic duct and common bile duct into the duodenum.

This reflex is found only on the palm of the right hand and the sole of the right foot. It is located just below the liver reflex in zone 3.

Oesophagus and stomach

The oesophagus is the food pipe that connects the pharynx to the stomach. Food passes into the stomach through the cardiac sphincter, a ring of muscle that prevents food re-entering the oesophagus when the stomach contracts.

The stomach lies in the upper part of the abdominal cavity, beneath the diaphragm. It is a J-shaped pouch into which food from the oesophagus passes. The stomach is lined with a mucous membrane containing thousands of microscopic gastric glands which secrete gastric juice and hydrochloric acid. The contraction of the stomach's muscular walls mixes the food with the gastric juices, breaking it down into a semi-solid mixture called chyme. Chyme is then passed into the duodenum (the first part of the small intestine) where further chemical digestion takes place.

The reflex to the oesophagus starts beneath the neck reflex in zone 1. It runs parallel to the spinal reflex until it reaches the stomach reflex. The stomach reflex is found on the soles of both feet and palms of both hands and is located between the diaphragm and the waist line. On the right foot and hand it covers zones 1 and 2: on the left foot and hand it covers zones 1, 2 and 3.

Spleen

This dark purple organ lying on the upper left side of the abdomen is the largest lymphoid organ in the body. In addition to producing lymphocytes, it removes bacteria by infiltration, removes and breaks down old and malformed red cells from the blood stream and serves as a reservoir for blood that can, if necessary, be used by the circulatory system.

The reflex for the spleen is found only on the sole of the left foot and the palm of the left hand. It is located in zones 4 and 5, below the diaphragm and above the waist line.

Kidneys

The kidneys are a pair of glands situated close to the spine in the upper part of the abdomen. They are deep maroon in colour and are surrounded by fat, which cushions and supports them. Their main function is the formation of urine, carried out by the nephrons that make up each kidney's interior. This process is vital to maintaining homeostasis and therefore life. Other key roles played by the kidneys are regulating the levels of many chemical substances in the blood; regulating the balance between the body's water and salt content; and helping to regulate blood pressure.

The reflex for the right kidney is found on the sole of the right foot and the palm of the right hand: the left kidney's reflex is on the palm of the left hand and the sole of the left foot. These reflexes are located in zones 2 and 3 at waist level.

Adrenal glands

See Orange for a description of these glands. Their position above the waist line means that they fall within that area of the body covered by the solar plexus chakra, so common ailments are covered in this chapter.

Treatment Colours
for Common Ailments

Nervous system

There are many conditions connected with the nervous system but only the ones that are quite straightforward to treat are listed here.

Shingles Shingles is the result of infection by herpes zoster, the virus responsible for chicken pox. During an attack of chicken pox the virus may find its way to the root of a nerve in the brain or spinal cord. Here it lies dormant, often for many years, until re-activated by emotional or physical stress. Shingles is a very painful condition that causes groups of blisters to form on the skin over the affected nerve.
To treat: For associated pain, use treatment colours indigo and its complementary gold to the relevant reflex(es). To treat the condition, apply turquoise and red/orange to the reflex(es). For example, if the shingles appear on the face, treat the face reflex.

Multiple sclerosis This degenerative condition may involve any part of the brain, the spinal cord or the optic nerves. Many nerves in the brain and spinal cord are enclosed in a protective covering called the myelin sheath. Multiple sclerosis is the inflammation of this sheath and affects a number of nerves in the central nervous system.
To treat: Treatment colours are violet and its complementary yellow through both feet.

Skeletal system

Ruptured or slipped disc In this condition the pulpy body at the centre of an intervertebral disc protrudes through a tear in the surrounding ligament.
To treat: Use treatment colours indigo and gold to the spinal reflex. This will relax the surrounding muscles and help ease the pain prior to seeing a chiropractor or osteopath.

Degenerative arthritis of the spine This condition is particularly common in those who do heavy manual work. It is characterized by degenerative changes to the intervertebral joints of the upper and lower back.
To treat: Treatment colours are yellow and its complementary violet to the spinal reflex.

Spondylitis This condition is sometimes known as ankylosing spondylitis or bamboo spine, and is caused by inflammation in the vertebrae. Its severity varies with each person. At its worst, it can result in total spinal stiffness.
To treat: Treatment colours are indigo and its complementary gold to the spinal reflex.

Fracture There are several types of fracture. These are: compound fracture, where the bone breaks through the skin; simple fracture, where the bone does not pierce the skin; complete fracture, where the bone fragments completely separate;

incomplete fracture, where the bone fragments are still partially joined.
To treat: After the fracture has been medically attended to, treat the appropriate reflex with yellow and its complementary violet.

Osteomyelitis This is the name given to bacterial infections of bone and marrow tissue. Because of bone's density, infection here is difficult to treat medically.
To treat: Treatment colours are red/orange and turquoise.

Osteoarthritis The cause of this is unknown but it is aggravated by wear and tear on the joints. The sites where it is most commonly found are the larger weight-bearing joints such as the spine, knees and hips.
To treat: Apply treatment colours yellow and its complementary violet to corresponding reflexes.

Rheumatoid arthritis The exact cause of this disease is unknown. The synovial membrane of a joint gradually becomes inflamed and swollen, leading to inflammation of other parts of the joint. This disease usually affects small joints such as the knuckles and toes, but it can affect other joints.
To treat: Apply treatment colours yellow with its complementary violet to the relevant reflexes.

Repetitive strain syndrome This is caused by repetitive motion of the wrist or other joints and can affect the wrist and thumb joints of practising reflexologists.
To treat: Apply treatment colours indigo and its complementary gold to the wrist or thumb joints.

Bursitis Bursas are found near joints and are soft, lubricating pads that minimize friction between body tissues. If a bursa is irritated by pressure, the small pad may become inflamed and filled with fluid, creating what is called bursitis. Joints particularly susceptible to this condition are knees, elbows, shoulders and the base of the big toe.
To treat: Apply treatment colours blue and its complementary orange to the relevant reflex.

Parathyroids

Hypoparathyroidism A condition in which the parathyroids are not producing sufficient hormones, resulting in the calcium level of the blood falling below normal. For this condition, it may help to spend a minimum of 20 minutes each day out of doors in natural daylight, to allow the light to enter the eyes. It is advisable to remove glasses or contact lenses.
To treat: Apply treatment colours yellow with its complementary violet to the parathyroid reflexes.

Hyperparathyroidism In this condition, an excessive amount of the parathyroid hormone is produced. There are several causes for this. The excess of calcium in the blood upsets the body's metabolism, resulting in indigestion and depression.

To treat: Apply treatment colours violet and its complementary yellow to the parathyroid reflexes.

Liver

Hepatitis Hepatitis is the name for inflammation of the liver. This condition can be caused by alcohol or drugs. A more serious form is caused by a bacterial or viral infection.

To treat: Treatment colours blue with its complementary orange should be used when this condition is caused by alcohol abuse or the use of drugs.

Cirrhosis This describes a degenerative liver condition where the liver is unable to regenerate its damaged tissue. One cause of this is alcohol abuse.

To treat: Apply treatment colours violet with its complementary yellow.

Toxicity The body can become toxic as a result of taking certain prescribed drugs, through drinking too much coffee or alcohol, or through following an unhealthy diet. The colours given below will help the liver to detoxify, but the underlying cause needs to be addressed. If the cause is the taking of prescribed drugs, it is important that the patient does not stop taking these unless advised to do so by his or her general practitioner.

To treat: Treatment colours are lime green and magenta.

Jaundice Jaundice comes from a word meaning yellow. If there is liver

inflammation or an obstruction in the bile duct, an increase of bilirubin will occur in the blood giving the skin and whites of the eyes a yellowish appearance. Jaundice can occur in premature babies, where it is the result of the immature liver's inability to cope with the output of bilirubin.

To treat: Treatment colours blue with its complementary orange should be administered through both feet or both hands.

Gall bladder

Gallstones These are usually crystallized bile pigment and calcium salts. It is estimated that by the age of 60 one in five women and one in twenty men have gallstones.

To treat: Treatment colours are orange with its complementary blue.

Oesophagus and stomach

Oesophagitis (inflammation of the gullet) The usual cause of this complaint is acid associated with hiatus hernia. Other causes include fungal infection and possible irritation from vomiting. The cause is usually diagnosed by oesophagoscopy.

To treat: Treatment colours are indigo with its complementary gold.

Functional dyspepsia or indigestion This could result from mental and physical stress such as anxiety, frustration, annoyance, physical fatigue from long hours of work, or loss of sleep. It may also be due to irritation of the digestive organs from eating too quickly without adequate chewing or from badly cooked or indigestible food.

To treat: Treatment colours are yellow with its complementary violet.

Gastritis This is characterized by inflammation of the stomach lining. Some of the causes are spicy food, an over-indulgence in alcohol, and taking certain drugs, such as aspirin.
To treat: Apply treatment colours indigo with its complementary gold to the stomach reflex.

Peptic ulcer An ulcer is a crater-like wound or sore in a membrane, and is a result of tissue destruction. A peptic ulcer can develop in the stomach, duodenum or oesophagus and the cause is thought to stem from a stressful lifestyle. Heavy smoking can aggravate this condition and slow down the healing process.
To treat: Apply treatment colours blue with its complementary orange to the stomach reflex.

Stomach cancer A malignant tumour. Such tumours have been linked to excessive alcohol consumption and to eating smoked or heavily preserved food.
To treat: Apply treatment colours magenta and lime green to the stomach reflex as well as through the soles of both feet or hands. This is given in conjunction with medical treatment. (See also Treating Cancer, page 98.)

Pancreas
Pancreatitis Acute pancreatitis is due to a sudden chemical reaction within the pancreas. It can occur in association with gall stones and particularly after heavy alcohol consumption.
To treat: Apply treatment colours indigo with its complementary gold to the pancreas reflex.

Diabetes mellitus This is caused by a deficiency, or total lack, of the pancreatic hormone insulin, made in the islets of langerhans. This lack results in a low absorption of glucose – both by the cells that need it for energy and by the liver that stores it. Consequently there will be an unacceptably high level of glucose in the blood.
To treat: Treatment colours are yellow with its complementary violet.

NB: If the person being treated is taking insulin, either by injection or in tablet form, it is important that they monitor their blood sugar levels during treatment.

Spleen
Enlarged spleen The spleen nearly always becomes enlarged as a symptom of another disorder. When enlarged it is prone to rupture and becomes overactive in removing certain types of cells from the blood.
To treat: Apply treatment colours yellow and its complementary violet to the spleenic reflex.

Low immunity The spleen acts as a filter for bacteria and other foreign substances. If it is not functioning to its full potential, we could succumb to bacterial infection.
To treat: Apply treatment colours turquoise and its complementary red/orange to the spleenic reflex.

Kidneys
Kidney stones These normally start as a tiny speck of solid matter deposited in the middle of the kidney, where urine collects before flowing into the ureter. As further deposits

cling to the original speck, a stone is formed. Very small stones are often carried away and passed in the urine, but larger stones, too big to pass down the ureter, remain in the kidney. If these need to be removed, a technique that uses ultra-sound pulverizes the stones so that they can be flushed out of the urinary tract.

To treat: Apply treatment colours orange and its complementary blue to the kidney reflex.

Nephritis This condition is also known as Bright's disease after Richard Bright, the man who first described it. Nephritis is inflammation of the kidneys and covers a group of diseases.

To treat: Apply treatment colours turquoise and its complementary red/orange to the kidneys.

Adrenal glands

Stress As a result of our physiological 'flight or fight' response to stress or anxiety, extra adrenaline is pumped into the circulatory system. If the adrenaline is not dispersed, through physical exercise for example, over time it can lead to a state of hypertension.

To treat: Apply treatment colours blue and its complementary orange through both feet.

Cushing's syndrome This is characterized by an excess of steroid hormones in the blood. In most cases it is caused by large doses of steroid drugs taken for other illnesses such as asthma or rheumatoid arthritis.

To treat: Apply treatment colours yellow and its complementary violet through either the feet or the hands.

Reflex	Condition	Treatment Colour	Complementary Colour
Nervous system	Shingles		
	Associated pain		
	Multiple sclerosis		
Skeletal system	Ruptured or slipped disc		
	Degenerative arthritis		
	Spondylitis		
	Fracture		
	Osteomyelitis		
	Osteoarthritis		
	Rheumatoid arthritis		
	Repetitive strain syndrome		
	Bursitis		
Parathyroids	Hypoparathyroidism		
	Hyperparathyroidism		
Liver	Hepatitis		
	Cirrhosis		
	Toxicity		
	Jaundice		
Gall bladder	Gallstones		
Oesophagus & Stomach	Oesophagitis		
	Functional dyspepsia		
	Gastritis		
	Peptic ulcer		
	Stomach cancer		
Pancreas	Pancreatitis		
	Diabetes mellitus		
Spleen	Enlarged spleen		
	Low immunity		
Kidneys	Kidney stones		
	Nephritis		
Adrenal glands	Stress		
	Cushing's syndrome		

The **Solar Plexus Chakra**

The Sanskrit name given to this chakra is 'Manipura' which means 'the jewel in the navel'. This is the fire centre, the focal point of heat, which radiates like a golden sun.

Linked to the solar plexus and, I believe, to the sacral chakra as well, is the 'Hara', a Japanese word meaning 'belly'. It is situated three fingers' width below the navel, close to the sacral chakra. Here we find the fire of Agni (the Hindu fire god) kindled. In oriental medicine the Hara is seen as the root and origin of Ki or vital energy and of the entire meridian system, which distributes Ki around the body. It is here that the work of digestion takes place to provide the body with heat and energy. In oriental medicine the relationship between health and a strong 'Hara' is an accepted fact.

The solar plexus chakra is situated between the twelfth thoracic and the first lumbar vertebrae. It is depicted as a bright yellow lotus flower with ten petals. In the centre of the lotus flower we find a downward-pointing red triangle with a T-shaped projection on each of its three sides. The animal present is the ram and the mantra or sound is RAM. Manipura is associated with the fire element and with the sense of taste.

The solar plexus chakra is the fire wheel and is associated with the sun and with the ego. It is a centre of vitality in the psychic and physical bodies because this is where prana (the upward-moving vitality) and apana (the downward-moving vitality) meet, generating the heat that is necessary to support life. When these two energies unite, this centre is awakened. Its polarity is power and powerlessness and when we are able to transcend this, the result is peace.

Manipura is linked with the astral or emotional body and, as well as responding to our feelings, it reacts to thoughts of worry, anxiety and fear. Physically, this centre is chiefly concerned with the process of digestion and absorption. The parts of the body that it influences are the skin, digestive organs, liver, gall bladder, stomach, duodenum and pancreas. The associated endocrine gland is the islets of langerhans, which form part of the pancreas.

When this chakra has excessive energy it can make a person judgemental, a workaholic, a perfectionist and resentful of authority. If it is depleted in energy we may lack confidence and worry what others think of us. We could suffer depression, insecurity and be in a state of confusion. We might also experience fear when alone and the discomfort of poor digestion. When the solar plexus chakra is balanced in energy, we enjoy good food, physical activity and show emotional warmth. We are also cheerful, outgoing, spontaneous, relaxed, uninhibited and have self-respect and respect for others.

Manipura interacts between the heart chakra and sacral chakra: if it is blocked, then sexuality is not connected to love. Only when the energy of this centre flows freely can a deep and fulfilling emotional life be experienced.

The solar plexus chakra on the feet and hands

The reflex for this chakra is found at the base of the metatarsal bone on the feet and along the metacarpal bone on the hands. To ascertain the state of this chakra, place your finger on the chakra's reflex point, on either the foot or hand, then with your other hand use a pendulum to dowse. If you find the chakra is over-active, treat with violet; if it is under-active, treat with yellow.

To treat, use either the reflexology torch with the appropriate coloured disc inserted, or place your finger on the reflex point and channel the required colour through that finger.

THE POSITION OF THE SOLAR PLEXUS CHAKRA REFLEX ON THE FEET AND HANDS

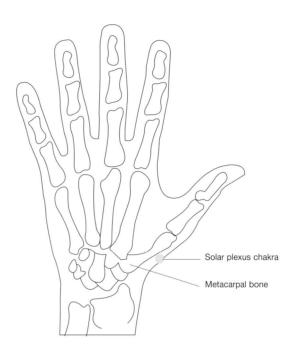

Solar plexus chakra

Metacarpal bone

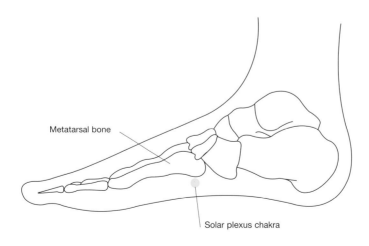

Metatarsal bone

Solar plexus chakra

Visualization
with **Yellow**

It is a warm summer's day and you are lying on a golden, sandy beach in a small cove. The sky is pale blue with tiny clouds scattered across its surface. The only sounds to be heard are the waves of the sea breaking gently on the shore. The atmosphere is one of peace and tranquillity.

Closing your eyes and releasing any thoughts from your mind, try to visualize your body as a mass of pulsating particles of energy constantly moving and flowing into harmonious patterns of light and sound waves. In appearance, the physical body appears to be dense and solid, but in truth it is in a perpetual state of motion as it vibrates to the rhythm and music of its dance.

Observing your body, take note of the places where the movement of energy appears to be slow or stagnant, creating patches of darkness. These can be caused by tension, stress, disease, pain or an unhealthy diet. Other causes are fear of the future, or insecurity stemming from early childhood. These are problems we have to face if we are to heal ourselves.

In the stillness and silence, feel yourself becoming detached from everyday life and its problems. In this state it is easy to look objectively at the problems preventing the free flow of your energy and to find a way of solving them. If you feel you have reached a crossroads in your life, ask your higher self to help you choose the path that is right for you.

Now visualize a yellow shaft of sunlight, filled with minute specks of brilliant white light, entering through the crown of your head. Mentally take this light to the parts of your body where you have discovered your energy to be slow or stagnant. Now imagine that energy's darkness being pierced by the yellow shafts of light, freeing the stuck energy and restoring harmony and balance so that these parts of your body again become part of the rhythm of the dance.

Finally, visualize shafts of yellow sunlight entering the soles of your feet to flood your body from your toes to the crown of your head. Then, as you exhale, allow this energizing light to pass through the pores of your skin into your aura. Cocooned in this yellow orb of sunlight, relax for as long as you wish.

Meditation with the Solar Plexus Chakra

Visualize a sunflower, taking particular notice of how large it is and how many petals it has. Look inside to its centre where deep golden stamens grow.

Take this flower into your solar plexus and allow its petals to become the rays of translucent light that radiate from our earthly sun. Feel the warmth that this is generating and the energizing effect it is having on your solar plexus chakra. This chakra is related to the element of fire and it is here that we must burn away any negativity and rid ourselves of old, irrelevant thought patterns.

While concentrating on this chakra, search within yourself for anything you need to change or to eliminate from your life and then think of ways of achieving this. Now allow the yellow light to radiate out to the rest of your body. Try to experience how it is affecting you mentally, emotionally, physically and spiritually. Do you feel attracted to or repelled by this colour? If you are attracted towards it, do you feel that you need its vibrations, or are you attracted to it because it is a colour that suits your complexion? If you are repelled by it, it could be because, at present, you don't need this colour for your well-being. If you have never liked this colour, the cause could stem from an event in your childhood that you found too painful to deal with and have buried in your unconscious mind.

To end this visualization, contemplate any insights you have gained into yourself.

Orange

Orange gained its name in the eleventh century from the Arabic word *naranj*, meaning 'fruit'.

Orange is a warm colour: it appears next to red on the colour spectrum but does not possess the vibrant heat of red. It is the main colour displayed by the hot spices used in Eastern countries, which verifies its connection with warmth and stimulation. Although it is an energizing colour, unlike red it contains the gentle, caring properties of the feminine energy. While it is not a complementary colour to red, orange is complementary to its energies, red being aligned with the masculine energy and orange with the feminine.

Like red, this colour is associated with sexuality and fruitfulness. The ancient custom of adorning brides with orange blossom was symbolic of this. In past eras orange pomegranate seeds were taken as an aphrodisiac.

Orange enhances our creative talents, generates joy, has the power to encourage freedom and movement on all levels. Its vitality is able to bring about a change in our biochemical structure, resulting in the dispersal of depression. Furthermore, its warm, invigorating nature makes it an emotional stimulant.

Orange is the dominant colour of the sacral chakra, and the endocrine glands associated with this chakra are the adrenals. In the aura, a bright clear orange denotes health and vitality; a deep orange, pride; a muddy, cloudy orange, a low intellect. A profusion of orange in the aura shows an abundance of vital dynamic force. The colour's negative attributes are pride and a leaning towards over-ambition.

The adrenal glands

The two adrenal glands are situated one on top of each kidney. They are yellowish in colour and consist of an outer cortex and an interior or medulla.

The cortex is responsible for secreting hormonal substances known as steroids. These are divided into three main groups. Group A consists of the mineral corticoids. These work on the tubules of the kidneys to help retain sodium and chloride in the body and to aid in the excretion of potassium. Group B consists of the gluco-corticoids. One of their functions is to assist in the conversion of carbohydrates into glycogen. The other hormones in this group are cortisone and hydrocortisone. The group C hormones are similar to those produced by the gonads. They influence growth and sex development in males and females.

The medulla of the adrenal glands secretes adrenaline and noradrenaline. Adrenaline stimulates the sympathetic nervous system: it also stimulates the liver into converting glycogen into glucose.

The reflexes for the adrenal glands are found on the soles of both feet and palms of both hands. They are located just above the waist line in zone 2, just above the kidney reflex. See the Yellow chapter for common ailments and their treatment.

Reflexes associated with the colour orange

Back of left hand

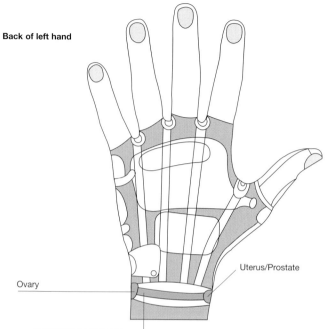

Ovary

Uterus/Prostate

Fallopian tube/Vas deferens

Back of right hand

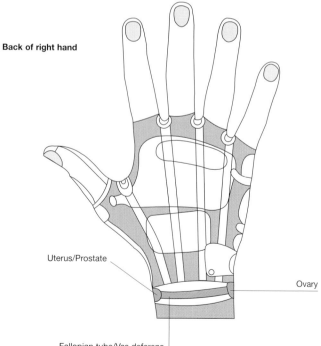

Uterus/Prostate

Ovary

Fallopian tube/Vas deferens

REFLEXES ASSOCIATED WITH THE COLOUR ORANGE

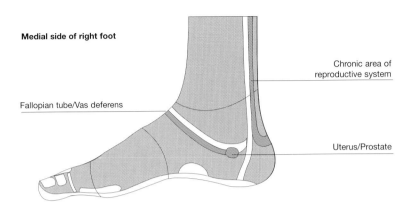

Medial side of right foot

Fallopian tube/Vas deferens

Chronic area of
reproductive system

Uterus/Prostate

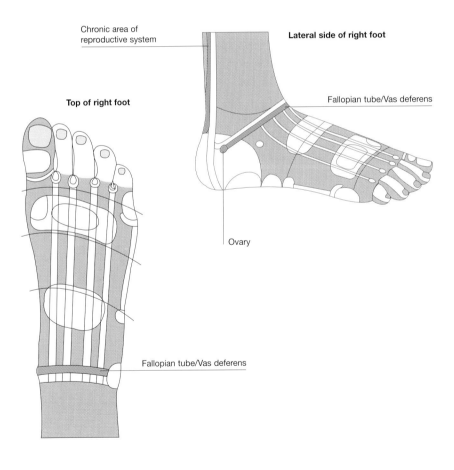

Chronic area of
reproductive system

Lateral side of right foot

Top of right foot

Fallopian tube/Vas deferens

Ovary

Fallopian tube/Vas deferens

Reflexes associated with the colour orange

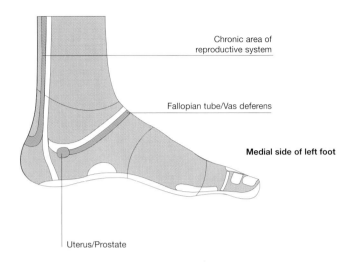

Chronic area of
reproductive system

Fallopian tube/Vas deferens

Medial side of left foot

Uterus/Prostate

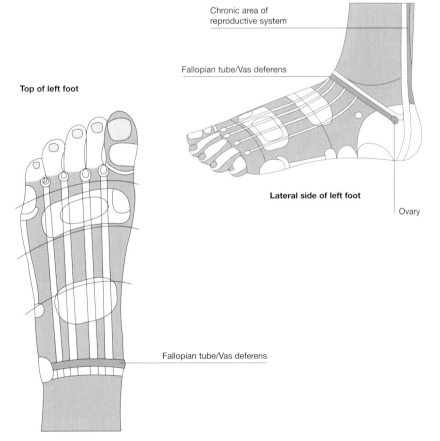

Chronic area of
reproductive system

Fallopian tube/Vas deferens

Top of left foot

Lateral side of left foot

Ovary

Fallopian tube/Vas deferens

REFLEXES ASSOCIATED WITH THE COLOUR ORANGE

Palm of left hand

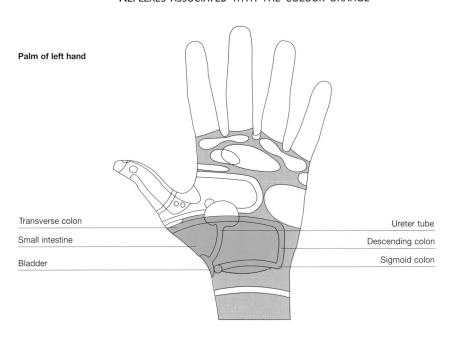

Transverse colon

Small intestine

Bladder

Ureter tube

Descending colon

Sigmoid colon

Sole of left foot

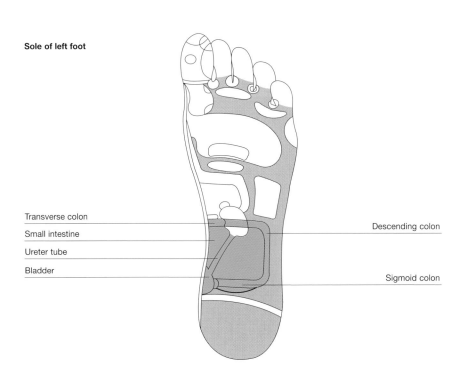

Transverse colon

Small intestine

Ureter tube

Bladder

Descending colon

Sigmoid colon

Reflexes associated with the colour orange

Palm of right hand

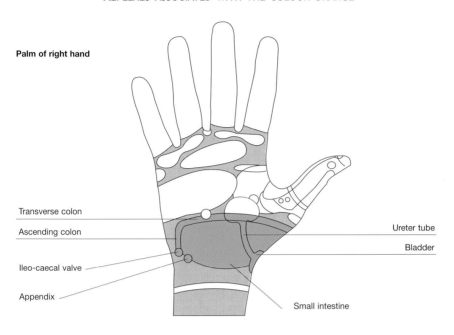

Transverse colon

Ascending colon

Ileo-caecal valve

Appendix

Ureter tube

Bladder

Small intestine

Sole of right foot

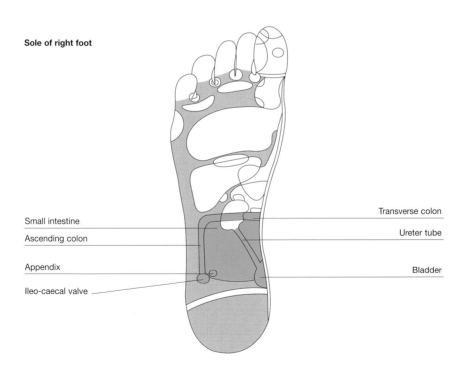

Small intestine

Ascending colon

Appendix

Ileo-caecal valve

Transverse colon

Ureter tube

Bladder

Associated Reflexes

Ureter tubes and bladder

The ureter tubes are narrow pipes which carry urine from the kidneys to the bladder. The bladder is a pear-shaped muscular sac which is a reservoir for urine. In a male the bladder lies in front of the rectum, but in a female it is separated from the rectum by the uterus and vagina. The bladder can contain up to 570 millilitres/20 fluid ounces of urine without being over-distended.

On the feet, the bladder reflex is found on the slightly puffy area on the medial side of both feet, at the top of the heel pad. From the bladder reflex, the ureter tube continues across zones 2 and 3, on the sole of the foot, to waist level. On the hands, it is located on the medial aspect of the right thumb, midway between the head of the metacarpal and the wrist joint. From the bladder reflex, the ureter runs upwards from zone 1, across zone 2, terminating just below the waist line.

Small intestine

Digestion is completed in the small intestine and virtually all absorption occurs there. The small intestine extends from the pyloric sphincter of the stomach to the first part of the large intestine, the caecum. It is approximately 6 metres/20 feet long and consists of the duodenum, the jejunum and the ileum. The duodenum, the beginning of the small intestine, is an area of great chemical activity and, in contrast to the acidity of the stomach, its environment is alkaline. The small intestine is richly lined with microscopic villi – finger-like projections – each villus having a rich network of blood capillaries that absorbs sugar and amino acids. At the base of the villi are glands which secrete intestinal juices.

The small intestine reflex, on the medial side of the feet, covers zones 1 to 4 from just below the waist line to just above the pad of the heel. On the hands it extends over zones 1 to 4 and covers the area of the metacarpal bones lying below the waist line.

Large intestine

In the colon the residual contents from the small intestine are gradually turned into faeces. The large intestine is approximately 1.5 metres/5 feet in length. The first part of this wide tube, the caecum, starts in the lower right abdomen. The ileum, the last part of the small intestine, enters the caecum at the ileo-caecal valve. The valve permits the contents of the ileum to enter the caecum but stops it back-flowing. Attached to the caecum is a worm-like tube, the appendix. From the caecum, the large intestine passes up the right side of the body to the underside of the liver. Here it turns left at the hepatic flexure and becomes the transverse colon. The transverse colon passes across the abdominal cavity to the spleen where, at the splenic flexure, it turns downwards to become the descending colon. This passes down the left side of the body and continues into the pelvic cavity where it becomes the sigmoid colon. The

sigmoid colon then passes into the rectum which opens to the exterior at the anus. This opening is guarded by the anal sphincter, which can be relaxed, when desired, to empty the rectum of its contents.

The reflex areas to the large intestine are found on the soles or palms of both feet and hands. The reflex area to the ascending colon is found in zones 4 and 5, over the tarsal or carpal bones, and extends up from this area to the waist line. The reflex for the transverse colon goes across at waist level, covering all five zones on the right and left feet or hands. On the left hand or foot, this reflex then continues down zones 4 and 5 for the descending colon. The reflex area to the sigmoid colon continues across the hand or foot to zone 1.

Ovaries

The ovaries lie in the lower part of the abdomen, one on each side of the uterus, and are the main female organs of reproduction. Their main hormonal secretions are oestrogen and progesterone. Each ovary is connected to the uterus by a fallopian tube. The ovaries contain thousands of eggs and each month, during a woman's fertile years, an egg is released into its fallopian tube and then slowly travels towards the uterus. If, on its journey, it is fertilized by a sperm, it will, on its arrival into the uterus, burrow into its soft, thick lining. If the egg is not fertilized, it is expelled from the body along with the uterine lining during menstruation.

The reflex area to the ovary is found on the outer side of the foot or hand, midway between the outer ankle bone and the back of the heel in the foot, or on the outer side of the back of the hand just above the wrist. The left and right ovaries are found on the left and right feet and hands respectively.

Uterus

The uterus is a hollow, pear-shaped organ whose walls are composed of powerful muscles. At the lower front end of the uterus lies the cervix, which leads into the top of the vagina. Its function is to house and protect a growing foetus.

The reflex area to the uterus is found on the inner side of the foot, midway between the ankle bone and the back of the heel, or on the inner side of the back of the hand just above the wrist.

Prostate gland

The prostate gland comprises a cluster of small glands surrounding the urethra at the point where it leaves the bladder. The exact function of this gland is unclear, but it is thought that the secretions produced by the prostate combine with the seminal fluid to stimulate the movement of the sperm after they have been ejaculated.

The reflex area to the prostate gland is on the inner side of the back of the hand just above the wrist, or on the inner side of the foot midway between the ankle bone and the back of the heel.

Treatment Colours
for Common Ailments

Bladder

Cystitis Cystitis, or inflammation of the bladder, is more common in women than in men because of the short female urethra which makes it much easier for infecting organisms to invade the bladder. The urethra may also become infected. The symptoms are pain or a burning sensation on passing urine, increased frequency and, sometimes, the presence of blood in the urine.

To treat: Treatment colours are red/orange with its complementary colour turquoise administered to the bladder reflex.

Cancer Cancer of the bladder is believed to be most common in men over 50. Malignant tumours spread within the walls of the bladder and may also spread to other parts of the body. The characteristic symptom of a bladder tumour is blood in the urine. It requires immediate medical investigation.

To treat: Treatment colours are magenta and lime green to the bladder reflex and through both feet. (See also the section on Treating Cancer, page 98.)

Bladder stones Stones that develop within the bladder tend to be larger than those that form in the kidneys and usually remain lodged there. These can cause troublesome symptoms and, if too large to pass through the urethra, they are normally removed surgically.

To treat: Treatment colours are orange and its complementary colour blue to the bladder reflex.

Small intestine

Crohn's disease This is a chronic inflammation of part of the digestive tract. The part most commonly affected is the ileum. The disease starts with patches of inflammation in the intestinal walls. These patches may grow or may spread from one part of the system to another. Diet plays an important role in controlling this disease.

To treat: Treatment colours are indigo and its complementary colour gold to the intestinal reflex.

Acute enteritis There are a number of infections which cause inflammation of part or all of the intestines, resulting in severe diarrhoea. Many attacks occur after eating contaminated food. When the organism enters the small intestine it multiplies rapidly causing diarrhoea and vomiting.

To treat: Treatment colours are red and its complementary colour green to the intestinal reflex.

Colon

Toxicity The colon can become toxic for many reasons, including constipation.

To treat: Treatment colours are lime green and its complementary colour magenta administered to the colon reflex.

Constipation Constipation implies that the bowels are being moved infrequently and with difficulty. Simple causes of constipation are low intake of food, a lack of fibre in the diet and a lack of exercise. Other causes could be taking prescribed medication, psychological disturbances (for example, depression) and irritable bowel syndrome.
To treat: Treatment colours are red with its complementary green.

Diarrhoea Acute diarrhoea is frequently caused by food poisoning. In this case, it is advisable not to treat with colour because the body is trying to rid itself of the damaging food as quickly as possible. If this condition is the result of nervous tension or fear, then it can be treated with the colours given. For continuing diarrhoea or diarrhoea alternating with constipation medical advice should be sought.
To treat: If caused through fear or nervous tension, the treatment colours are blue with its complementary orange to the colon reflex.

Irritable bowel syndrome With this condition the bowel rhythm is disturbed, resulting in alternating diarrhoea and constipation, abdominal pain and muscular spasm of the colon. IBS can be caused by nervous stress or may result from an attack of enteritis. Heavy smoking is thought to accentuate the symptoms.
To treat: Treatment colours are

orange with its complementary blue to the colon reflex, and for pain, indigo and gold through both feet.
Diverticulitis This is characterized by inflammation of one of the pouches present in the large colon of a diverticulosis sufferer. The inflammation is frequently caused by a small piece of hard faeces becoming lodged in the pouch.
To treat: Alongside medical treatment, the treatment colours red/orange and its complementary turquoise are used.

Appendicitis This is characterized by an inflamed and infected appendix. If you suspect a patient has this condition, it is important that immediate medical help is sought. With this condition there is a risk of the appendix rupturing, leading to peritonitis.
To treat: After the removal of the appendix, the scar tissue can be treated with yellow and its complementary violet.

Cancer of the colon The abnormal cells that form with this condition can produce either an ulcerous area that bleeds easily or a constriction that blocks the passage of faeces. It is thought that one cause of this condition could be a highly refined/low fibre diet.
To treat: Treatment colours are magenta and lime green to the colon and through both feet. (See also the section on Treating Cancer, page 98.)

Ovaries

Ovarian cyst This is a sac full of fluid which grows on or near an ovary. It can grow to a considerable size.
To treat: Treatment colours are orange with its complementary blue to the ovary reflex.

Premenstrual tension This is characterized by water retention, headache, emotional tension and a bloated feeling. In women who suffer from PMT it usually starts a week before menstruation. This condition can be associated with a progesterone deficiency.
To treat: Treatment colours are orange with its complementary blue to the ovary reflex.

Also, check for any imbalances in the chakra reflexes found along the spinal reflex.

Uterus

Fibroids A fibroid is a benign tumour growing either on the outside or within the uterus's muscular wall and attached to the uterus by a thin stalk. Normally there is more than one fibroid.
To treat: Treatment colours are orange with its complementary blue to the uterus reflex.

Dysmenorrhoea This is a cramp-like pain that can occur during the first two days of menstruation and is sometimes associated with hormonal imbalance.
To treat: Treatment colours are indigo and gold through the uterus reflex. Also check the chakra reflexes for imbalances.

Pelvic infection Infection of the genital tract is very common, and a variety of organisms can be responsible. If you suspect that your patient may have this condition, he or she needs to be encouraged to see their doctor to ascertain its cause.
To treat: Treatment colours are red/orange with its complementary turquoise given alongside medical treatment.

Cervical erosion A cervical erosion is an extension of columnar epithelium (a delicate mucus-secreting tissue that lines the canal of the cervix) to some of the cervix's outer parts. Here it becomes susceptible to infection.
To treat: Treatment colours are violet and its complementary yellow to the uterus reflex.

Prostate

Enlarged prostate It is believed that all men over the age of 45 have some enlargement of the prostate. This is a natural result of the ageing process. In some men the prostate gland becomes stiff and inflexible. As the gland becomes more rigid and the muscles of the bladder are unable to compensate for this, the urethral exit becomes restricted and the flow of urine obstructed. When this happens, medical intervention is necessary.
To treat: Treatment colours are blue with its complementary orange (this is for an enlarged prostate that is not restricting the flow of urine).

Prostatitis Prostatitis is inflammation of the prostate gland and is usually the result of a urinary-tract infection.
To treat: Treatment colours are red/orange and its complementary turquoise to the prostate reflex.

Reflex	Condition	Treatment Colour	Complementary Colour
Bladder	Cystitis		
	Cancer		
	Bladder stones		
Small Intestine	Crohn's disease		
	Acute enteritis		
Colon	Toxicity		
	Constipation		
	Diarrhoea		
	Irritable bowel syndrome Associated pain		
	Diverticulitis		
	Appendicitis (to scar tissue)		
	Cancer		
Ovaries	Ovarian cyst		
	Premenstrual tension Check chakra points for imbalances		
Uterus	Fibroids		
	Dysmenorrhoea Check chakra points for imbalances		
	Pelvic Infection		
	Cervical erosion		
Prostate	Enlarged prostate		
	Prostatitis		

The Sacral Chakra

The Sanskrit name for this chakra is 'Svadisthana' meaning 'one's own abode'. It is situated just below the navel and is shown with six petals radiating its dominant colour, orange. Inside the petals is a crescent moon, which houses a *makara*. This is a legendary animal, similar to an alligator, which bears the characteristics of the fish, the crocodile and the elephant. The white crescent moon is the symbol of female receptivity. This chakra is associated with the water element and affects the flow of fluids in our physical body. The mantra or sound that it resonates to is VAM.

All water is associated with the Great Mother and the feminine principle. Water is said to be the liquid counterpart of light and the source of all potentialities in existence. Water has the power to dissolve, abolish, purify and regenerate. It is associated with our emotions – 'the tears of joy or the tears of sorrow'.

Water has the great ability to flow freely when uninhibited. The challenge this centre presents, therefore, is ascertaining whether or not we are flowing with the energies of life. We need to ask ourselves if we are holding on to old emotions that may be hindering us, and if we have cleared away the old patterns and genetic traits that act as large boulders, preventing the free flow of all aspects of our being.

The sacral chakra is the source of vitality for the etheric body. It influences our feelings of sexuality and governs our love/hate relationships. Its polarity is attraction and repulsion, likes and dislikes. To transcend this chakra is to rise above our likes and dislikes and to see all things as part of the whole.

This is a very powerful centre in controlling a person's sex life and, normally, the centre does not awaken until puberty. Sexual energy is the second most powerful energy in a human being, the first being the Shakti energy located in the base chakra. Svadisthana has a close connection with the creative energies at the throat chakra, which displays its complementary colour, blue.

This chakra governs the female reproductive organs, the mammary glands, the skin and the kidneys: its associated endocrine glands are the adrenals. An explanation for the adrenal glands can be found in the sections relating to the colour yellow.

When this chakra is functioning to its full potential, a person's intuitive powers are opened and their sensitivity heightened. When Svadisthana is in a state of balance, a person is friendly, optimistic, shows concern for others, has balanced sexual energy and a sense of belonging. When the chakra becomes blocked and deficient in energy, a person could become resentful, distrustful, oversensitive, extremely shy and fearful. If it becomes over-charged, a person can become aggressive, manipulative, obsessed with sex and emotionally explosive.

When Svadisthana is not functioning to its full potential, the physical symptoms that can arise are dysfunction in either the male or female reproductive organs, intestinal complaints, bladder and kidney disorders, circulatory problems, low energy, disturbances of the central nervous system, migraines and irritability.

The sacral chakra reflex on the feet and hands

The reflex for this chakra is found at the top of the navicular bone on the feet and at the base of the metacarpal bone on the thumb. To ascertain if this chakra is in balance, place your finger on the chakra's reflex point, on either the foot or hand, and then with your other hand use a pendulum to dowse. If you find the chakra is over-active, treat with blue, if it is under-active, treat with orange.

To treat, use either the reflexology torch with the appropriate coloured disc inserted, or place your finger on the reflex point and channel the required colour through that finger.

THE POSITION OF THE SACRAL CHAKRA REFLEX ON THE FEET AND HANDS

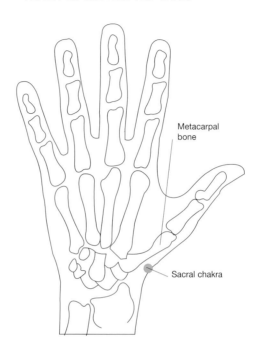

Metacarpal bone

Sacral chakra

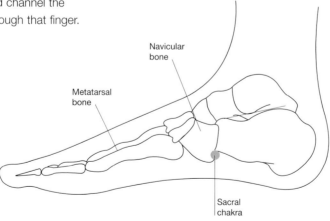

Navicular bone

Metatarsal bone

Sacral chakra

Visualization with Orange

For this visualization you will need a bowl containing five or six oranges. Sit in a place where you can clearly see the oranges and start your visualization by just looking at them. Observe how they have been placed in the bowl. Are they all the same size? Is their colour uniform or does it vary? Do they have a scent? Is the texture of the skin the same for each orange, or does it differ?

After contemplating the bowl of oranges for about 10 minutes, take one of them into your hands. Carefully look for any variation in the colour or texture of the skin. Now cut the orange open and note the difference in colour between the skin and the flesh. Place half the orange in the palm of your left hand and hold the palm of your right hand approximately 5 centimetres/2 inches above it. Close your eyes and try to feel the vibration of this colour through the chakra in the palm of your right hand.

Breathe in the scent and see if it provokes any memories of past events which you may have forgotten. If your mind is stimulated to remember past occurrences, try to relive them. If they were happy events, re-experience the joy and happiness they brought you: if they were sad, look at any lessons they may have taught you. When you feel you have experienced all that you can, return the half orange to the bowl.

Feeling the stillness and peace surrounding you, bring your awareness into your sacral chakra, situated just below the umbilical scar. Visualize this as a marigold with petals created from orange light, each petal shimmering as it intertwines its vibrant orange light with the other colours that are present in your aura. Slowly start to breathe in orange, bringing it from the earth up into this chakra and experiencing the energy and joy that the colour is giving you. Visualize the organs in your lower abdomen responding to, and being energized by, this colour – the colour they vibrate to. Allow any depression that you may have been feeling to be dissolved. Before ending this visualization, take a few moments to contemplate anything this colour has taught you.

Meditation with the Sacral Chakra

Picture yourself sitting amidst a range of mountains whose summits are veiled in a light, diaphanous vapour woven through with golden threads of light radiating from the rising sun. No sound disturbs the breathless quietude but the sound of water as it cascades down from the mountain top into the pool by which you are sitting. The turbulence created by the power of the water, as it enters the pool, forms a large cavern which appears to reach deep into the bowels of the earth. The tiny droplets that bounce from the water's surface sparkle like many-faceted diamonds and create tiny rainbows of light as they fall back again to merge with the pond's tumultuous uproar.

The energy created by the cascading water's power can be likened to the energy this chakra, when it is in balance, gives to the physical body. The turbulence created is akin to our unstable and fluctuating emotions, which can cause our bodies dis-ease and stress. The great Eastern sage, Patanjali, equated our feelings and thoughts to a pond across whose surface stones were constantly being skimmed, creating ripples which prevent us from seeing the pond's floor. It is only when one stops throwing the stones that the pond's floor comes into view. Similarly, if we are not in control of our thoughts and feelings, they mask the light and peace of our inner self.

Water, the element connected with this chakra, has the power both to create and destroy. Water is linked to our emotions and to our bodily fluids.

We are able to release our emotions through our tears but, if we are unable to cry, our emotions build up, like the water behind a dam, until they eventually break the physical body.

Before ending this meditation, think about the energy this chakra is able to give you when it is in a stable condition. Now imagine the pool by which you are sitting becoming still and silent as the cascade of water ceases. Looking into its surface you see a reflection of yourself – and the stillness and tranquillity of the smooth, calm water becomes instilled into this reflection.

Red

Red has the longest wavelengths and lowest energy of all visible light. Its situation next to infra-red on the electromagnetic spectrum associates red with warmth. In the Victorian era, at night, when heating was often restricted to the kitchen, it was customary to wear a red nightshirt to help maintain body temperature.

The names associated with the varying shades of red are derived from the colour's source. Vermilion is taken from the ancient name for mercuric sulphide; cinnabar, crimson and carmine are taken from the Latin *kermesius*, the name of the dye extracted from the kermes insect; and ruby red comes from the root of the *Rubia tinctoria* plant. Ruby red was considered a most exclusive dye which made it very expensive.

When we focus on red, the lens of the eye has to adjust and this gives the impression that the object is closer than it truly is. For this reason, a room decorated in red will appear smaller than its actual size. This power of constriction makes red unsuitable for asthmatics.

Red is a colour with aggressive qualities and these link it with the masculine energy, and with war and combat. It is also the symbol of life, strength and vitality, and is associated with the heart and circulatory system, thus connecting it with love, sexuality and the arousal of sexual energy. Our forefathers believed that blood held the secret of life, and this accredited the colour with special powers. Certain Native American tribes daubed their corpses with red ochre to symbolize both their continued existence in the spirit world and their eventual return to earthly life.

Red is related to the base chakra, and the endocrine gland associated with this chakra is located in the testes. In the aura a clear, bright red shows generosity, ambition and

Testes

The testes contain the endocrine gland associated with the base chakra. They lie just below the abdomen in the scrotal sac. The testes are positioned outside the body because the formation of spermatozoa requires a temperature slightly lower than that found in the abdomen. The main bulk of the adult testis is made up of the tubular system that produces spermatozoa. Spermatozoa formed in the tubules take approximately three months to mature, after which they are stored in the seminal vesicles, beside the prostate. The endocrine portion of the testis consists of the cells that secrete the male hormone, testosterone. These cells also produce small amounts of oestrogen. Testosterone is the hormone responsible for changing a boy's body into a man's.

The reflex for the testicles lies midway between the outer ankle bone and the back of the heel. The right testis is located on the right foot and the left testis on the left foot. On the hands it is located on the outer border of the back of the hand, at the top of the ulna.

affection; a profusion of red means strong physical propensities; dark red indicates deep passion, love, courage, hatred and anger; a reddish-brown shows sensuality and voluptuousness; a cloudy red points to greed and cruelty, and crimson reveals lower passions and desires. The darker shades of this colour are usually associated with the adverse side of love – lust. This connection is illustrated in such phrases as 'scarlet woman'.

Red has exciting and stimulating properties. But it is also a colour that has contra-indications when used in therapy. It quickens the heart rate, increases the blood circulation and activates the release of adrenaline. This makes it a colour that should be used with caution on anyone suffering heart problems, circulatory problems, high blood pressure, anxiety and emotional disturbances. According to Hunt's book *The Seven Keys to Colour Healing,* red splits the ferric salt crystals into iron and salt. The red corpuscles in the blood absorb the iron and the salt is eliminated by the kidneys and the skin. Hunt believes that this ability makes red a good colour with which to treat anaemia or iron deficiency.

Red's ability to increase the blood circulation makes it ideal for treating viral or bacterial infections. Flooding an infected area with red light will increase the blood supply to that area enabling the blood's white corpuscles to deal more quickly with the invading bacteria or virus.

Reflexes associated with the colour red

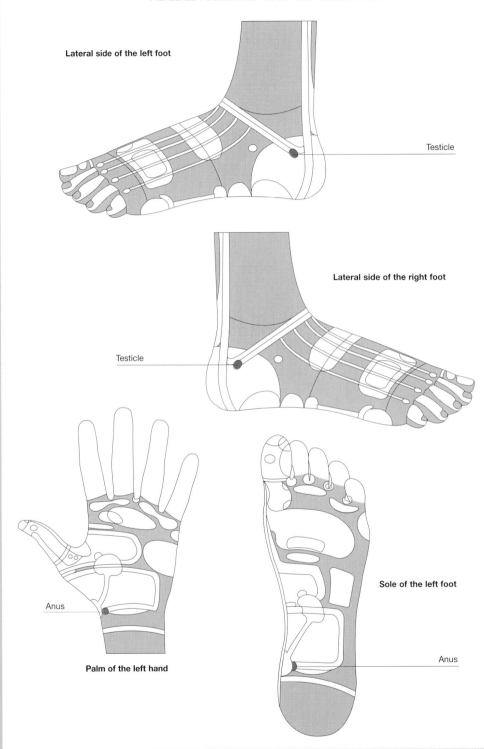

Lateral side of the left foot

Testicle

Lateral side of the right foot

Testicle

Anus

Palm of the left hand

Sole of the left foot

Anus

REFLEXES ASSOCIATED WITH THE COLOUR RED

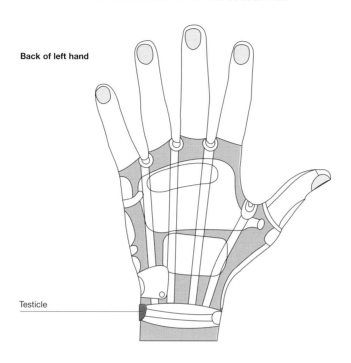

Back of left hand

Testicle

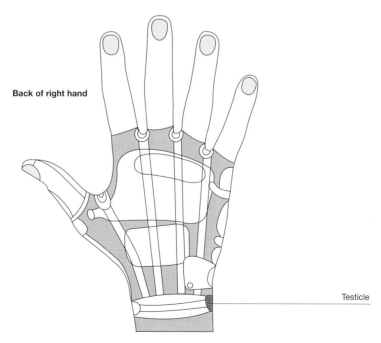

Back of right hand

Testicle

Associated Reflexes

Anus

The anus consists of a tube approximately 4 centimetres/1½ inches long leading from the rectum through a ring of muscles to the anal orifice. This orifice is kept closed by the external and internal sphincter muscles, which are under the control of a nerve centre in the spinal cord.

The reflex for the anus is found only on the left foot and the left hand. It is located in zone 1 on the medial side of the sole of the foot and the palm of the hand, at the end of the reflex for the rectum.

The feet and lower legs have no reflexes on the feet or hands. In these cases treat the actual feet and legs.

Legs

The legs are connected to the trunk of the body by the hip or pelvic girdle, which consists of two large pelvic bones, one located on each side of the pelvis. These two bones, together with the sacrum and coccyx, provide a strong support for the torso, as well as connecting the legs to the axial skeleton. The bones comprising each leg are the femur, the patella (kneecap), the tibia and the fibula. When patients attend with minor leg problems, I treat the leg itself.

Feet

The feet are a mirror image of the whole body, The aura which surrounds our physical body is also mirrored on our feet, so whenever we treat the feet we are also working with the aura. Each foot contains twenty-six bones and thirty-three articulations joined together by over 100 ligaments. These bones are the calcaneus, the talus, the navicular, the cuboid, three cuneiform bones, five metatarsals and fourteen phalanges. The talus is the only foot bone that articulates with the fibula and tibia bones of the leg. When a person is walking, the talus initially bears the entire weight of the body. Part of this weight is then transmitted to the calcaneus and the remainder to the other tarsal bones. The heel bone or calcaneus is the largest and strongest bone in the foot.

The bones of the feet are arranged in such a way that they form two arches – the longitudinal and the transverse – which enable the foot to support the weight of the body and provide leverage while walking. The bones which make up these arches are held in position by tendons and ligaments. If these tendons and ligaments are weakened, the height of the medial longitudinal arch may decrease or fall. This results in a flat foot. If the medial longitudinal arch is abnormally elevated, usually the result of a muscle imbalance, a condition known as clawfoot occurs.

The muscles of the foot are intricate and are used for support and locomotion.

Comfortable and properly functioning feet are essential for the well-being of the whole body. Painful, abnormal feet can lead to bad posture, fatigue, muscular cramp and backache. It is therefore important that your feet should be kept in good condition. Hard skin should be removed and the nails kept short. If the nail of the big toe is too long and presses into the side of the toe (the head reflex) headaches can occur.

Wearing ill-fitting shoes can deform the feet. This is detrimental to health because the reflexes that occur at the site of the deformity are affected. Ideally we should walk barefoot whenever possible, allowing the feet to move freely and the skin to breathe.

Before carrying out a reflexology treatment, observation of the feet should be made. The things to consider are the temperature; any abnormalities in the bone structure; the colour of the skin. These could give an indication of disease in the body. For example, an alteration in the tone of the skin beneath the phalanges of the second and third toes could indicate an eye problem; hard skin, corns or calluses over a reflex could reveal a problem in the corresponding part of the body. The more you practise this visual art, the more you will come to realize how much information can be gleaned about a person through the condition of the feet.

THE BONE STRUCTURE OF THE FOOT

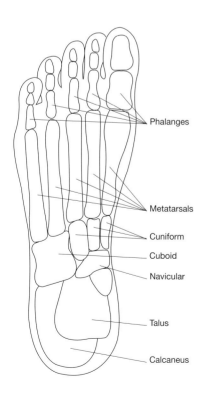

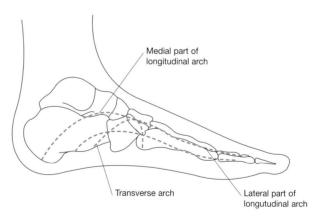

THE ARCH OF THE FOOT

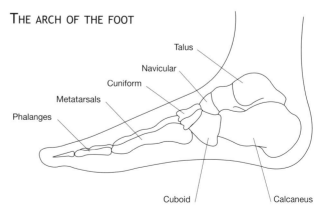

Treatment Colours
for Common Ailments

Testes

Cysts of the epididymis Cysts of the epididymis are very common in men over the age of 40. Although the cysts tend to grow because sperm accumulate within them, they are thought to be harmless.

To treat: Treatment colours are magenta and its complementary lime green to the testicle reflex.

Testicular cancer Cancer occurring in the cells of a testis is said to be one of the most easily cured types of cancer if the condition is medically treated in its early stages The main symptom is a lump in the affected testicle.

To treat: Treatment colours are magenta with its complementary lime green to the testicle reflex. (See also the section on Treating Cancer, page 98.)

Anus

Haemorrhoids Haemorrhoids are anal varicose veins and can be termed internal or external. An internal haemorrhoid occurs near the beginning of the anal canal. A haemorrhoid close to the anal orifice is considered to be external.

To treat: Treatment colours are yellow with its complementary violet to the anal reflex.

Anal fissure An anal fissure is a small ulcer or break in the skin in the region of the anal canal. The main symptom is an unpleasant burning pain, particularly with a bowel movement – a pain that can persist for some time.

To treat: Treatment colours are indigo with its complementary gold. (These two colours are used to help alleviate any pain. For this condition, it is advisable to seek medical advice.)

Legs

Varicose ulcers Varicose ulcers can be caused by poor circulation and oedema, which is a collection of fluid in the leg or legs. Consequently, any small injury to the skin is unlikely to heal quickly because the tissues are filled with stagnant fluid. As a result, the minor abrasion on the leg enlarges and finally becomes an ulcer – a flat area where the skin surface breaks down to leave a pale, weeping centre.

Dr Marta Fenyo, a biophysicist, laser specialist and inventor from Budapest, worked with Professor Endre Mester in researching the effect of soft laser light on leg ulcers, bedsores and varicose veins. Later she began experimenting to find out which component in laser light was responsible for the healing process. The answer she came up with was polarized light (see page 34).

From the work of Fenyo and a man called John Stephenson came the discovery that polarized light boosts the immune system and has a dramatic healing effect on varicose ulcers.

I have found the use of polarized light invaluable for treating this leg condition and scar tissue. Polarized light lamps can be obtained from The Glowing Health Company. Their address is at the back of this book.

To treat: Treatment colours are yellow with its complementary colour violet to the leg if you do not possess a polarized light machine.

Feet

Corns and calluses These are areas of skin that have thickened because of constant pressure. Corns are small and develop on the toes or fingers and calluses are larger and develop on the soles of the feet. Pressure on either causes tenderness in the underlying tissue and adversely affects the associated reflex.

To treat: Try to eliminate the underlying cause (for example badly fitting shoes) and treat the affected

areas with a corn file to cut away the upper layers and ease the discomfort.

Verrucas A verruca is a common wart which develops on the sole of the foot. It is produced by a virus. Verrucas are contagious and are spread by touch or by contact with the shed skin of the wart.

To treat: Treatment colours are red/orange with its complementary turquoise to the affected area.

Athlete's foot This is a harmless condition caused by a fungus that grows in the skin between and under the toes. The fungus may also affect other parts of the foot and the nails.

To treat: Treatment colours are violet with its complementary yellow to the affected area.

Reflex	Condition	Treatment Colour	Complementary Colour
Testes	Cysts of the epididymis		
	Testicular cancer		
Anus	Haemorrhoids		
	Anal fissure		
Legs	Varicose ulcers		
Feet	Verrucas		
	Athlete's foot		

The Base Chakra

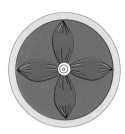

The Sanskrit name for this chakra is 'Muladhara', *mula* meaning 'root' and *ardhara* meaning 'base' or 'support'. It is connected to the earth element and the sense of smell. Muladhara is situated at the base of the spine and is depicted with four red petals. Inside the petals is a yellow square representing the earth element and stability. Radiating out from the square are six spears: these project from the four corners and from the middle of the sides. The spears represent the many paths that are open to us as we travel along life's road. The animal associated with this chakra is the elephant with seven trunks. The elephant is a slow, heavy animal and, at this chakra, it symbolizes our need to be grounded and the wisdom of walking along our chosen spiritual path slowly and with care. His seven trunks are believed to signify the minerals we need to sustain physical life: they also represent the seven chakras and their dominant colours. Sitting above the elephant is a red, downward-pointing triangle, signifying the feminine aspect of creation. Within the triangle is a phallus or lingam, around which is coiled the *kundalini* or serpent power. Above the phallus is a small crescent moon representing the divine source of all creation. The mantra or sound which this chakra resonates to is LAM.

The base chakra has a very close connection with the physical body, providing it with vitality and strength. It is connected with our survival instinct and is responsible for integrating us with the earth. Its polarity is the incoming and outgoing breath. To transcend this chakra one needs to work at rising above animal survival instincts.

This chakra is the seat of the *kundalini* or serpent fire. The esoteric spine houses a thread composed of three strands of energy. These three strands are known as the *pingala*, the *ida* and the *sushumna*. The *ida* is the negative strand: it relates to the path of consciousness and psychic unfoldment and is connected to the parasympathetic nervous system. The *pingala* is the positive strand: this channels the dynamic energy of prana and is associated with the sympathetic nervous system. The third thread is the *sushumna* and is the path of pure spirit, providing a channel for the rising of the *kundalini*, the great spiritual energy force. These three paths channel electric fire, solar fire and fire by friction. The *kundalini* fire is the union of these three fires and only when a person has reached a certain stage of spiritual development can this energy be raised safely and rapidly.

Excessive energy in this chakra can make a person aggressive, egoistic and domineering. Deficient energy here makes a person uninterested in sex and ungrounded. It can create depression, a lack of confidence and insufficient will power to achieve one's aims in life. But when this chakra is balanced, a person is grounded and centred, master of themselves and sexually affectionate: also, vitality is provided for the physical body, creating a sense of well-being.

Some of the physical symptoms

that could manifest when this chakra is not functioning to its full potential are testicular disorders, inhibited rejuvenation of blood cells, haemorrhoids and spinal and leg problems.

The base chakra reflex on the feet and hands

The reflex for this chakra is found at the lower back edge of the calcaneum on the feet and at the bulbous part of the radius on the hands. To ascertain whether this chakra is in balance, place your finger on the chakra's reflex point on either the foot or hand, and then, with your other hand, use a pendulum to dowse. If you find the chakra is over-active, treat with green; if it is under-active, treat with red.

To treat, use either the reflexology torch with the appropriate coloured disc inserted, or place your finger on the reflex point and channel the required colour through that finger.

THE POSITION OF THE BASE CHAKRA REFLEX ON THE FEET AND HANDS

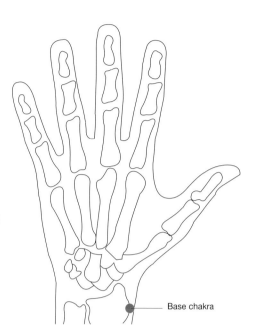

Base chakra

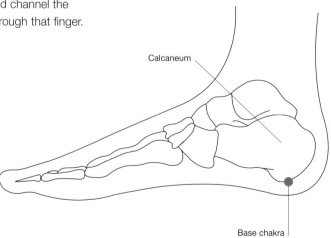

Calcaneum

Base chakra

Visualization with Red

It is a cold winter's evening and the world is wrapped in her dark mantle of night. Stars, filling the clear, deep indigo sky, resemble tiny candle flames that provide light for the deep vaults of heaven. As the starlight sheds its rays on to the frost-covered ground, each tiny water crystal reflects the light and sparkles like a many-faceted diamond. As you hurry through the frosty streets, towards your home, your hands and feet tingle with the cold, even though they are protected with warm clothing, and your face, which is just visible above the collar of your thick winter's coat, feels numb.

Upon reaching your home, you open the front door and walk through into the hall, where you remove your outdoor clothing. You then go into the sitting-room and are greeted by the

glow of the log fire burning in the hearth. Sitting down on the hearthrug, you relish the warmth of the fire as it penetrates your chilled body and, looking into the fire, you watch the flames, clothed in wispy, pale grey, swirling smoke, as they dance and intertwine with each other. Look at the flames' varying shades of red, occasionally intermingled with deep shades of orange and very narrow streaks of blue.

As you concentrate upon these flames you feel them inviting you to become one of them. You accept and, in so doing, they allow you to feel the warm, deeply energizing and earthing colour of red. As you dance to the rhythm of their dance, your body flows with the freedom of molten lava and all heaviness, tension and strain is dissolved. The deep shades of orange fill you with joy and awaken your creativity, and you feel the need to take this experience and to share it with others.

Returning from this meditation, contemplate ways in which you can share your experience with others. There are many people in the world who long for the warmth and joy of true friendship and there are others who are waiting for their own inner flame of light to be re-kindled. Sometimes, all we need to do to help those around us is just to be. If we are able to radiate from ourselves the peace and joy of our own inner light then it will be felt and will affect those with whom we come into contact. Take a few moments to reflect on these thoughts.

Meditation with the Base Chakra

Bring your awareness into your spine, visualizing this as a beautiful column of golden light. As you do so, imagine that you are standing outside your base chakra. This is large enough for you to enter by the door which opens in front of you. As you walk inside, you find yourself in a circular room. The walls and ceiling appear to be made from a soft, white, gossamer material and upon the floor lies a deep-piled white carpet. At the centre of this room a red rose bud floats upon a small, shallow pond.

Walking up to the bud, gently touch its soft, outer petals and watch as it slowly starts to open. When it has fully opened, you find at its centre a deep red ruby. The flower is large enough and strong enough for you to go and sit at its centre, next to the ruby. As you sit down on the soft petals, your body becomes engulfed in the ruby's red rays.

At first, this colour makes you feel uncomfortable because it has a tendency to make your body feel heavy and restricted. You also become conscious of the heat the colour is producing and the vibrant energy it is sending through your body.

Lying back against the flower's petals and looking up at the ceiling, you notice a circular hole through which you can see other rooms beyond the one in which you are sitting. Each room seems to be displaying a different colour, and each is linked to the others by a golden thread of light which penetrates its centre. As you contemplate what you are being shown, you realize that the room in which you are sitting is your foundation – the foundation both for your spiritual life and for your work as a complementary practitioner. If this foundation is strong and vibrant, like the colour it is displaying, then you will be able to ascend safely through the shaft of golden light into the rooms above, where greater knowledge and insights can be gained. Creating a strong foundation in whatever we do can be hard work, but it is necessary if we are to grow and proceed safely along our chosen path.

In ending this meditation, think about your own foundation in life and any physical, emotional, mental or spiritual changes this colour has engendered in you.

Turquoise

The seven colours associated with the major chakras have been covered in the preceding chapters. The colours that are discussed on the following pages are those additional colours that make up the twelve-colour wheel, but which are not connected with a major chakra. (See pages 44–45.)

Turquoise, comprising blue and green, is the last colour to appear out of the blue end of the spectrum. The proportion of the two colours involved determines it as blue or green turquoise.

In esoteric teaching, the endocrine gland associated with the heart chakra is the thymus. The thymus gland contains one of the minor chakras and this chakra radiates turquoise, taking blue from the throat chakra and green from the heart chakra. The thymus gland forms part of the immune system, which makes turquoise a good colour for boosting that system.

Turquoise is the national colour of Persia, the country where some of the oldest and finest turquoise gemstones originate. The ancient Persians called these gemstones *piruesh,* meaning 'joy' and believed that their colour could 'ward off the evil eye', giving protection to their animals as well as to themselves.

The cooling properties of turquoise make it a good colour for treating inflammation, especially when it is used in conjunction with its complementary red/orange. When red/orange is administered to a part of the body, it increases the blood supply to that area. Blood contains white corpuscles which are responsible for destroying bacteria, therefore red/orange deals with the infection and turquoise brings down the inflammation.

Other colours used in colour reflexology

Rose pink: This, the colour of unconditional love, is created when white is added to red. A gentle, nurturing colour related to the heart chakra, it is used on a physical level where red is contra-indicated. On an emotional level it is used with violet for those suffering loss in love. Violet mends the broken heart and rose pink replaces the pain and trauma with unconditional love.

Pearl: This colour clears stagnant energy from the aura's etheric layer. Applied to the solar plexus it benefits abdominal complaints resulting from emotional imbalances and stress. Applied to the throat chakra and spleen reflexes it disperses blockages or disharmonies in the etheric body.

Silver: This colour's shiny appearance mirrors our own personality and state of being. The silver ray has cleansing, cutting and burning qualities and is rarely used in the colour/reflexology combination. It is used mainly, and only by qualified practitioners, for cases of obsession.

REFLEXES ASSOCIATED WITH THE COLOUR TURQUOISE

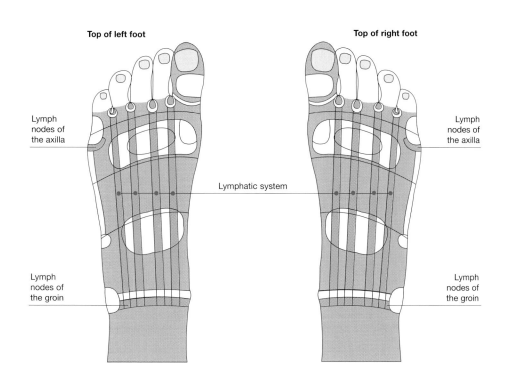

Top of left foot

Top of right foot

Lymph nodes of the axilla

Lymph nodes of the axilla

Lymphatic system

Lymph nodes of the groin

Lymph nodes of the groin

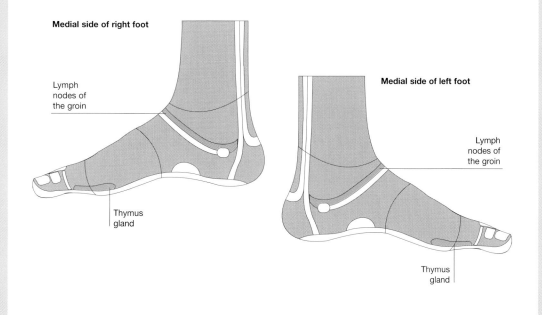

Medial side of right foot

Lymph nodes of the groin

Thymus gland

Medial side of left foot

Lymph nodes of the groin

Thymus gland

REFLEXES ASSOCIATED WITH THE COLOUR TURQUOISE

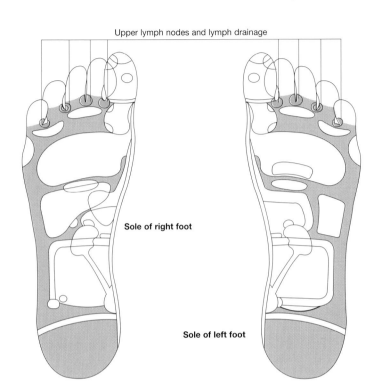

Upper lymph nodes and lymph drainage

Sole of right foot

Sole of left foot

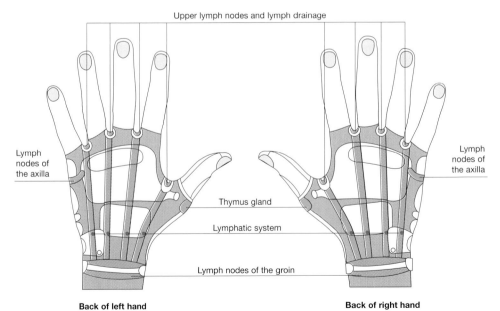

Upper lymph nodes and lymph drainage

Lymph nodes of the axilla

Lymph nodes of the axilla

Thymus gland

Lymphatic system

Lymph nodes of the groin

Back of left hand

Back of right hand

Associated Reflexes

Lymphatic system

Our immune defences against infection depend primarily on the lymphatic system. This system consists of lymphatic vessels that transport lymph (the name given to tissue fluid once it has entered the lymphatic vessels) to the groups of lymph nodes widely distributed throughout the body.

The lymphatic vessels unite to form larger channels which ultimately rejoin the general circulatory system. These larger lymphatic vessels resemble small veins in structure and are provided with valves to prevent back-flow.

As the lymph is transported around the body it is filtered by lymph nodes. These are located in clusters along the pathway of lymphatic vessels. The lymph nodes, together with other lymphatic tissue (in the spleen and the tonsils, for example), produce lymphocytes, which have various functions, including the production of antibodies and attacking foreign and abnormal cells.

The thymus, a small lymphoid tissue organ, is important in determining the character of lymphocytes (especially in early infancy and childhood) so that they do not attack the body's own tissue, but are ready to recognize and destroy invaders. The thymus is the dominant gland of the heart chakra and is described in Green (see page 94).

The lymph nodes that are easily accessed on the feet and hands are those to the groin, the breast, the upper lymph nodes to the neck and the lymph nodes of the axilla (situated in the armpit).

The reflex areas to the lymphatic system are situated on the backs of the hand and tops of the feet. These reflexes extend from the webs of the fingers down to the wrist or from the webs of the toes up towards the ankle bones.

The reflex for the lymph nodes to the groin is located in all five zones across the back of the wrists, and across the top of the feet between the ankle bones and around the outer and inner ankle bones.

The reflex for the axilla lymph nodes is positioned on the outer edge of the feet and hands, just below the shoulder reflex.

The remaining reflexes for the lymph are located on the tops of the feet and backs of the hands and run in straight lines between the web of each toe and finger to just over the top of the ankle and wrist bones. Pressure exerted between the webs of the toes or fingers allows for lymph drainage.

Treating the reflex areas to the lymphatic system on either the feet or hands – especially the lymph nodes nearest the site of infection – is important when there is infection present in the body.

When treating a patient who is experiencing a retention of bodily fluids, all the lymphatic reflexes should be treated. In cases of infection or fluid retention, it can be beneficial to re-treat the lymphatic system on both the feet and hands at the end of a reflexology treatment.

Treatment Colours
for Common Ailments

Lymphatic system

Allergy An allergy is a physical disorder caused by hypersensitivity of the immune system to substances that are eaten, inhaled or injected.
To treat: Work with lime green and magenta to the lymphatic reflexes.

Immuno-deficiencies Immuno-deficiency is a breakdown in the body's ability to defend itself against infection. It usually occurs as a result of some other disease.
To treat: Treatment colours are turquoise and its complementary red/orange to the lymphatic reflexes.

Lymphoma A lymphoma is a form of malignant tumour caused when a lymphocyte in a lymph gland begins to multiply uncontrollably.
To treat: Treatment colours are magenta and its complementary lime green to the lymphatic reflexes and also through both feet.

AIDS Acquired Immune Deficiency Syndrome is a life-threatening disease but one that many complementary therapists work with, especially if they work in care centres for AIDS sufferers. AIDS is an infectious disease transmitted by a virus (the human immuno-deficiency virus HIV) and spread by contact with bodily fluids. When treating this disease care must be taken. If there are open wounds on the feet, treat the hands.
To treat: Treatment colours are turquoise and red/orange to the lymphatic reflexes, then flooding both feet with violet and yellow.

Infection in the body
To treat: Where there is infection in any part of the body (for example a cold, or a septic finger) apply turquoise with its complementary red/orange to the lymphatic reflexes after treating the infection with the specified colour.

Reflex	Condition	Treatment Colour	Complementary Colour
Lymphatic system	Allergy		
	Immuno-deficiencies		
	Lymphoma		
	AIDS		
	Infection		

Visualization
with Turquoise

In your imagination, take yourself to a place where you are surrounded by mountains, their peaks soaring up towards the heavens. The summits of the tallest peaks lie under a blanket of freshly fallen snow which glistens in the light of the winter sun. The snow's softness and radiance are in marked contrast to the barren starkness and mighty power of the mountains.

Finding a gentle, undulating path, you start to walk along it up into the mountains. As you ascend, the atmosphere grows colder and you become aware of the noise made by your boots as you walk over loose, rocky pebbles.

Walking on, you hear the sound of water, and soon you see a tiny waterfall cascading over the rocks and boulders down to a meadow stream in the valley below. Where the sun catches the water, rainbows appear. Continuing past the waterfall you notice an entrance in the side of the mountain. On investigation, you discover this to be a cave, and you walk inside.

At first the cave's interior appears dark and airless but, as your eyes become adjusted to the darkness, you see that you are surrounded by stalagmites and stalactites which create a variety of beautifully shaped sculptures across the cave's floor and ceiling. When you look more closely at the floor of the cave, you find that it is covered with turquoise stones of all shapes and sizes. Finding a ledge in the rock, sit down and pick up some of these pieces of turquoise, placing them in your lap. Taking each stone in turn, examine its subtle variations of colour. Then place it on the palm of your left or right hand and hold the palm of the other hand approximately 3 centimetres/1½ inches above it.

Concentrating on your hands, try to feel the energy emanating from the piece of turquoise you are holding. Becoming aware of this energy tends to take practice because it involves sensitizing the minor chakra situated in the palm of each hand.

Now place the stone you are holding on any part of your body which you feel would benefit. Sense the stone's vibration bringing this part of your body back into balance. Feel it strengthening and energizing your immune system. Lastly, place the turquoise over your thymus gland and visualize the stone activating the minor chakra situated there.

Now remove your boots and socks and, sitting very quietly, feel the energies from the turquoise which lies scattered on the ground entering your body through the minor chakra situated on the sole of each foot. Reflect how this energy is affecting you mentally, physically and emotionally.

To end this visualization, imagine yourself surrounded by an orb of protective turquoise light.

If you have a piece of turquoise, you can hold it, or place it beneath one of your feet, while you work with this visualization.

Red/Orange

Red/orange is made up of equal quantities of red and orange. It lies between the strong, vibrant, red, masculine energy and the gentler, softer, orange, female energy. The combination of male and female energies in red/orange creates wholeness and harmony. When used in therapy, spectral red carries contra-indications (which have been given in the section of the book dealing with red) but in some cases, red/orange can be used where red cannot.

Similar to red, red/orange is a warm colour and has the ability to activate the circulatory system. For this reason it is used with its complementary turquoise for combating infection.

To experience the subtle differences between red and red/orange, try the following exercise. You can work with the two coloured squares shown below or, if you are able to find gels (the material used as filters for stage lighting) in these two colours, then work with the gels.

Another way of working to experience these two colours is to find flowers or autumn leaves which display them. Place your hand in turn around the red flower or leaf and then the red/orange flower or leaf, and attempt to feel the subtle difference in their energies.

Exercise

To work with the coloured squares, first cover the red/orange square with a piece of plain white paper. Then gaze at the red square in order for the red rays to be absorbed through your eyes. After approximately 3 minutes, repeat with the red/orange square. Now close your eyes and try to sense the subtle difference between the two colours.

If you are working with gels, place the red gel in front of your eyes and look through it for approximately 3 minutes, then replace it with the red/orange gel. Using gels is the more powerful of the two techniques.

Red

Red/orange

Gold

The colour gold is warm and lustrous and has good light-reflecting properties. It is derived from mixing together yellow and orange and is complementary to indigo.

Gold is associated with mysticism and symbolizes universal spirit in its perfect purity. It is a colour which possesses numerous religious connotations through its association with divinity and with saints (in religious art, it is used to depict the halo around saints' heads). Gold is connected with all the sun gods, and with the gods and goddesses associated with the ripening of the harvest. To Zeus is attributed the golden cord upon which the universe is said to have hung – the 'rope of heaven' on which all things are threaded. Athena, the daughter of Zeus, is reported to have worn a golden robe. In Hinduism, gold represents immortality, light and truth. It is the fire of Agni, the Hindu fire god and one of their three great deities.

The ancient Egyptians attributed gold to the sun god, Ra. The Incas referred to gold as 'the blood of the sun'. In alchemy gold is looked upon as the sun's essence.

In Western medicine, gold has long been used for various arthritic and rheumatic conditions, for spinal problems and for tuberculosis. In homoeopathy it is a remedy for depression and suicidal tendencies. Anthroposophic medicine claims that gold improves circulation, increases body warmth and makes a good salve for lupus. I believe that, in reflexology, gold applied to the spinal reflex revitalizes the nervous system; applied to the spleenic reflex it can revitalize the body.

Visualization with Gold

Imagining that you are sitting quietly in the countryside, visualize the sun as a round ball of molten gold reflecting its light over your surroundings. As you inhale deeply, imagine that you are taking in, through the crown of your head, one of the sun's reflected rays of light.

Imagine this bright golden light travelling through your spinal column, energizing the spinal cord and all the nerves that branch from it to your body's various organs and muscles. Then, as you exhale, picture this colour travelling through the numerous *nadis* present in the etheric layer of your aura. Repeat this breathing exercise nine more times.

On your eleventh inhalation, take the golden shaft of light down from the crown of your head into your spleen and, as you exhale, visualize the colour extending from the two minor chakras connected with your spleen to each of your seven major chakras. Repeat this a further nine times and, with each repetition, visualize each of your chakras becoming a miniature sun of molten gold which brings warmth and vitality both to your physical body and your aura.

Magenta

Magenta is produced by combining red and violet, colours which sit at opposite ends of the spectrum. Magenta dye was first produced by the French, who called it *fuchsine* after the fuchsia plant. Some years later the Italians renamed it magenta, after one of their villages near which a bloody battle had been fought.

Past decades have had their own name for this colour. In the 1930s it was called 'shocking pink'; in the 1950s 'hot pink'; in the 1960s 'kinky pink'. All these names describe it as a bright, exciting, fun colour, but it has also been portrayed as voluptuous and sensuous.

Psychologically, magenta enables us to let go of the old emotional and mental patterns which stand in the way of our spiritual growth. If we hold on to ideas and conditioning which originated in our childhood or adolescence, we become fixed and rigid: this prevents us from growing and evolving. Letting go of conditioning can prove difficult because it involves change, which can cause insecurity and uncertainty.

Allowing changes to occur, so that we can flow with the energies of life, destroys our habitual patterns and routines. This can be unsettling for our personality, but for our spirit it is bliss because it can move unhindered towards the vision which it had before incarnating into a physical body. Once we have incarnated, this vision is lost to our normal senses through conditioning, but our spirit remembers and will pursue its mission at all costs.

Both red and violet lie next to the burning rays of infra-red and ultra-violet, giving magenta the power to work with cancer on the physical level.

Visualization with Magenta

Picture before your inner eye a golden circle. Inside this circle is a beautiful magnolia flower, in full bloom and nestled in a bed of mid-green leaves. In the magnolia's petals white and varying shades of magenta intertwine. Inside the flower are golden stamens, heavy with pollen. The early morning dew that has formed on the flower's petals glistens in the sunlight that is heralding the start of a new day.

As you concentrate on the magnolia flower, visualize it increasing in size until its petals enfold you and you are sitting at its centre.

Be still for a moment and try to feel the softness of the flower's petals. Be conscious of the soft glow of magenta light that radiates from them and surrounds you. As you sit in the warmth generated by this colour, feel it releasing any physical tension. Now look at any emotional or mental problems which are bothering you and try to find a way of resolving them. Feel this colour giving you the strength to let go of any conditioning that is preventing you from evolving as a human being. If you are at a crossroads in your life, let go of any anxiety concerning the direction you

should take, for by so doing it is often possible to see more clearly which path we are meant to choose.

Having mentally looked at all the conditioning and attachments that are holding you back, look up to the top of the flower and notice the halo of magenta light encircling it. Become aware of the way in which the magenta halo gently fades into the white light which was born out of the sacred darkness and which contains all things. As you gaze into the white light, imagine that you are being drawn up into it.

White is the colour of purity but it is also a colour that signifies change. The reason why a bride wore a white dress was a sign of her purity and the change she was making in leaving the home of her parents to live with her husband. In Eastern countries white is the colour of mourning, symbolizing the fact that the dead person's spirit has left its earthly home and returned to spirit.

As you relax in the white light, allow it to penetrate the hidden depths of your emotions and thoughts to uncover anything you may still be holding on to. When you feel you have delved into yourself as far as you can, visualize the light as a liquid which washes and cleanses all aspects of your being. When your cleansing is complete, move back down into the pale magenta light so that it can fill you with unconditional love.

To end this meditation, gently begin to return to everyday consciousness. Allow the petals of the magnolia to get smaller and smaller until you are once again sitting outside it and it becomes a picture before your inner eye.

Visualization with Lime Green

Lime green is the complementary colour to magenta, and its properties are described on page 94. To familiarize yourself with this colour, work with this visualization.

It is a warm, sunny, spring day and the buds on the trees have opened to reveal the various shades of lime green. Against the darker green displayed by the grass, the lime green leaves look fresh, clean and youthful.

Imagine that you are sitting on the grass, under the trees. As the sun's rays filter through the leaves, they cloak you in an orb of lime green light. This is a colour which invites you to examine any negative thoughts or feelings that you may be harbouring so that these can be changed to thoughts of a positive nature. Any negativity surrounding our life could attract to us negative energy from the surrounding atmosphere. In time, this could create an imbalance in the physical body which would eventually manifest as a physical disease.

Try working with the following affirmation: today, all my negative thoughts and feelings will be replaced by positive ones.

Self-Help with Colour

When practitioners treat people with reflexology and colour, they should, I feel, also help them to use colour to help themselves. Practitioners also need to develop the capacity to work with themselves. Obviously, diet plays a huge part in the self-help process, because basically, we are what we eat. The human body is a very beautiful piece of machinery which is self-repairing, given the right conditions. If we become the owner of a new car, we make sure that it is filled with the correct petrol and oil. Such is the case with our own body. If we fuel it with healthy food and liquid it will serve us well and we will be filled with energy.

Similarly, we can help ourselves with colour. We need to remember that we are surrounded with colour, which is continually changing according to our mood and state of health. Each organ, muscle and bone in the physical body vibrates to a set frequency. If the vibrational frequency in part of the body changes, thereby causing disease, it can be restored by introducing the correct colour frequency and by finding and working with the cause that brought about the vibrational change.

Each of us needs to feel responsible for our own health and well-being. It is all too easy to describe our set of symptoms to a doctor and be given pills or medicine. This process, however, does not allow us to tune into our own bodies in order to find out what has caused the disease and then to rectify it so that the body can return to harmony and health. All of this does

take effort, initiative and time, but the whole process can become one of learning and evolving. By this process, we are also able to help others when they have problems. Drawing on experience can be far more beneficial than working from intellectual knowledge alone.

Some of the ways in which practitioners and their patients can help themselves are given below.

The use of coloured silk or cotton

For this, a piece of body-length silk or pure cotton approximately 2 x 0.5 metres/6 x 2 feet is needed. Ideally this should be coloured with natural dye. (Dyes made out of natural ingredients are more harmonious to the body's vibrations.) When using the material, the person needs to be dressed completely in white or, if they are in the privacy of their own home, they can be naked. Lying in a warm, sunny or brightly lit room, the body is covered with the silk or cotton, in the required colour, for 20 minutes. Because each cell of the body is light sensitive, during this time it is able to absorb the colour.

If working with colours at the red end of the spectrum it is recommended that this procedure is carried out first thing in the morning: these are stimulating colours and so evening use could cause insomnia.

Another way of working is to place a piece of silk or cotton, in the colour required, over the part of the body that is suffering disease. For an infected finger, try placing a piece of red/orange cotton over it for an hour and then change to a piece of turquoise cotton for the same length of time.

The use of coloured clothing

Because each cell of our body is light sensitive, the colour of the clothes we wear also affects us. It can be beneficial to wear a piece of clothing in the colour we currently need. If the coloured garment is a blouse, shirt or dress, again, whatever is worn underneath must be white. If we choose to wear underwear in the appropriate colour, then it is necessary to wear white on top. (This is not always practical, alas, because coloured underwear tends to show through the white garment worn over it.) As our colour sensitivity develops, we begin to know intuitively which colour we need.

Unfortunately, it make take some trial and perseverance to find appropriately coloured clothes because the fashion industry tends to dictate which colours and patterns we should wear for any given season of the year.

The use of gemstones

Healing with crystals is reputed to be a very ancient therapy. In his book *Exploring Atlantis*, Dr Frank Alper traces the therapy back to Atlantean times, when, he says, the large temples devoted to healing had domed roofs constructed from quartz crystal which refracted the light and filled the temples with the spectral colours.

One method of using gems is to apply one of an appropriate colour to the part of the body which is unwell or to the energy centre which is malfunctioning. For example, amethyst followed by rose quartz can be placed on the heart centre of someone suffering from a 'broken heart'.

Solarising quartz crystal is a method with which I have worked. This can be done by putting a quartz crystal on top of a piece of stained glass (in the required colour) placed over a lamp. The lamp is then switched on for about 10 minutes. The colour from the stained glass impregnates the crystal and the crystal amplifies the colour's energy. The solarised crystal can then be placed on any part of the body which needs that particular colour. (For further information on this and other solarisation techniques – water, sac lac tablets and cream – see pages 50–51).

Quartz crystal is used in the reflexology torch because of its power to intensify the energy of the colour being used. When working with crystals in this way, they must be cleansed after each colour infusion, otherwise the energies of the colour which has just been used will intermingle with those of the new colour. The crystal torch is cleansed by shining ordinary torchlight through it for a few seconds after each colour used.

At the end of the day, the head of the crystal torch is immersed in sea-salt water and left overnight. Next day it is rinsed under running water. Ordinary crystals which have been colour solarised should also be placed in salt water after use.

Colour breathing

With this method, the colour needed is visualized and inhaled into the diseased part of the body. The red, red/orange, orange, gold and yellow rays are brought into the body through the feet; the green and lime green rays are brought in horizontally through the heart centre; the blue, turquoise, indigo, violet and magenta rays are breathed in through the top of the head. The colour is then visualized permeating that part of the body which needs it. If, for example, someone was suffering from a headache, then indigo would be visualized permeating the top of, and flooding, all parts of the head.

When practising breathing exercises, it is important not to retain the in or out breath for longer than a count of two. Yogic breath retention is used primarily to move body energies – a technique which should be practised only under instruction from a qualified yoga teacher.

Exercise

Colour breathing is also an excellent method for balancing and revitalizing the chakras.

To do this, sit somewhere quiet, where you will not be disturbed. Begin by quietening your mind and relaxing your body.

Then, on your next inhalation, visualize a shaft of pure red light coming up from the earth, into your feet and into the base chakra. As you exhale, allow the colour to radiate out into your aura. This process is repeated three times with each colour and its chakra.

Next visualize a shaft of pure orange light rising from the earth to enter into your feet and your sacral chakra. Breathe this colour out into your aura. Try to experience the joy and energy that this colour brings to your body, mind and spirit.

When you are ready, breathe a shaft of yellow light in through your feet and up into your solar plexus chakra. Visualize this chakra becoming like a radiant golden sun with its energizing, healing rays touching every part of your body. As you exhale, visualize the sun's rays extending into your aura.

On your next inhalation, bring a shaft of green light horizontally into your heart chakra. As it flows into your aura on your next exhalation, feel every part of you being brought into balance.

Now visualize a shaft of blue light entering through the top of your head, into your throat chakra. Exhaling, allow this colour to flow into your aura to surround you with a cloak of peace and protection.

When you are ready, inhale a shaft of deep indigo light through the top of your head and into your brow chakra. Feel this colour radiating deep relaxation as it flows into your aura on your next exhalation.

Finally, visualize a shaft of violet light entering through the top of your head into your crown chakra and, as you exhale, allow this colour to flow into the aura around your head.

Before ending this exercise, spend a few moments visualizing the beautiful coat of many colours that you have just woven around yourself.

Useful Addresses

Pauline Wills
The Oracle School of Colour
9 Wyndale Avenue
Kingsbury
London, NW9 9PT
E-mail:
Pauline@oracleschool.fsnet.co.uk
(Information on courses and
products including the reflexology
crystal torch)

Dorothye Parker
Colour Resonance School
28 Devonshire Road
Bognor Regis
West Sussex, PO21 2SY
E-mail: Dorothy-parker@hotmail.co

Primrose Cooper
The Meridian Centre
6 Larnach Close
Uckfield
East Sussex, TH22 1TH
Tel/fax: (01825) 762964

Lilian Verner-Bonds
The Colour-Bonds Association
77 Holders Hill Drive
Hendon, NW4 1NN
Tel/Fax: (020) 8349 3299

**The Maitreya School of
Colour Healing**
33 Shaftesbury Road
London, N19 4QW
Tel: (020) 7272 2981

**International Association
of Colour**
46 Cottenham Road
Histon
Cambridge, CB4 9ES
Tel: (01223) 563403

**The Colour Association of
the United States**
589 Eighth Avenue
New York 10018-3005
USA

The Bayly School of Reflexology
Monks Orchard
Whitbourne
Worcester WR6 5RB
Tel: (01886) 821207
Fax: (01886) 822017

**Complementary Medical
Association**
The Meridian
142a Greenwich High Road
London, SE10 8NN
Tel: (020) 8305 9571

**Lynda Jackson –
Macmillan Centre**
Mount Vernon Hospital
Rickmansworth Road
Northwood
Middlesex, HA6 2RN
Tel: (01923) 844014

**The Glowing Health
Company Ltd**
Jaysforde House
College Road
Newton Abbot,
Devon, TQ12 1EF
Tel: (01626) 336337

SAD Lightbox Co. Ltd
Unit 1 Riverside Business Centre
Victoria Street
High Wycombe
Bucks, HP11 2LT
Tel (01494) 526051
Fax (01494) 527005

Bibliography

Allanach, Alan, Colour Me Healing: Colourpuncture, A New Medicine of Light, Element Books, 1997.

Alper, Frank, Exploring Atlantis, Arizona Metaphysical Society, 1981.

Anodea, Judith, Wheels of Life – A Users Guide To The Chakra System, Llewellyn Publications, 1987.

Birren, Faber, Colour Psychology and Colour Therapy, Citadel Press, 1950.

Birren, Faber, The Symbolism of Colour, Citadel Press, 1998.

Fitzgerald, William H and Bowers, Edwin F, Zone Therapy, Health Research, Mokelumne Hill, CA, 1917.

Gerber, Richard, Vibrational Medicine, Bear & Co., 1998.

Ghadiali, Dinsaha P, Spectro-Chrome Metry Encyclopaedia (3 volumes), Spectro-Chrome Institute, Malaga, 1933.

Hall, Nicola M., Reflexology – A Way To Better Health, Gateway Books, 1988.

Hall, Nicola, Reflexology for Women, Thorsons, 1994.

Hunt, Ronald, The Eighth Key to Colour, L N Fowler & Co. Ltd, 1965.

Ingham, Eunice, Stories the Feet Can Tell Thru Reflexology, Ingham Publishing, 1951.

Ingham, Eunice, Stories the Feet Have Told Thru Reflexology, Ingham Publishing, 1951.

Kunz, Dora (ed.), Spiritual Aspects of the Healing Arts, The Theosophical Publishing House, 1985.

Libermann, Jacob, Light: Medicine of the Future, Bear & Co., 1991.

Libermann, Jacob, Take Off Your Glasses and See, Thorsons, 1995.

Lorber, Jakob, The Healing Power of Sunlight, Merkur Publishing, 1997.

Macpherson, G (Ed.), Black's Medical Dictionary, 1995.

Parker, Dorothye, Colour Decoder, Barron's, 2001.

St Pierre, Gaston and Boater, Debbie, The Metamorphic Technique, Element Books, 1982.

Thibodeau/Patton, The Human Body in Health & Disease, Mosby, 1997.

Tortora, Gerard J and Anagnostakos, Nicholas P, Principles of Anatomy and Physiology, Harper Collins, 1990.

Verner Bonds, Lilian, Colour Healing, Lorenz Books, 1999.

Verner Bonds, Lilian, Discover the Magic of Colour, Optima, 1993.

Weiser, Samuel, The Healing Power of Light, 2001.

Wills, Pauline, Colour Healing, Piatkus, 1998.

Wills, Pauline, Colour Therapy, Element Books, 1993.

Wills, Pauline, The Colour Healing Manual, Piatkus, 2000.

Wills, Pauline, The Reflexology Manual, Eddison Sadd, 1995.

Wills, Pauline, Visualisation, Headway, 1994.

Wright, A, Beginner's Guide to Colour Psychology, Kyle Cathie Ltd, 1995.

Picture Credits

Chrysalis Books: 46, 47, 49, 50, 55, 79.

Digital Vision: front cover (image of back), 6, 32, 62, 66, 69, 73, 78, 100, 104, 105, 117, 119, 120, 124, 125, 132, 135, 140, 141, 148, 153, 159, 162, 166.

Neil Sutherland: 91, 93, 152.

Science Photo Library: 28 (Mark de Fraeye), 29 (National Library of Medicine), 30 (Jean-Loup Charmet), 35 (John Greim), 36 (David Parker), 40 (Ganon Hutchings), 112 (Roger Harris).

All diagrams by **Andrew Easton**.

Index

About the Author

Pauline Wills originally trained as a dental nurse and worked for many years in private practice. During this time she took up the study of yoga with an Indian Master. After qualifying, she worked as a yoga instructor at evening institutes. She then went on to train as a reflexologist with the Bayly School of Reflexology and as a colour practitioner with the Maitreya School of Colour Healing. In 1990 she pioneered the integration of colour with reflexology.

Feeling the need for freedom to teach the knowledge accumulated and experience gained over the years, in 1998 she founded the Oracle School of Colour based in north west London, a school which is affiliated to the Complementary Medical Association in the UK. Here she works as a reflexologist and colour practitioner, teaches the integration of colour with reflexology and conducts a two-year Colour Practitioner Diploma course. She also continues to teach yoga. She has travelled internationally, conducting courses on colour therapy and on the integration of colour with reflexology.

During the past six years she has authored several books on colour, on reflexology and on the integration of these two therapies.